COOKIES
to die for!

COOKIES
to die for!

BEV SHAFFER

Food Photography and Food Styling by
JOHN R. SHAFFER

PELICAN PUBLISHING COMPANY
Gretna 2009

To my mom, Olga, who taught me to love baking and to create with my hands
("I just had *to put apricot filling in the kiflis, Mom!")*

The word "Pelican" and the depiction of a pelican are trademarks
of Pelican Publishing Company, Inc., and are registered in the
U.S. Patent and Trademark Office.

Library of Congress Cataloging-in-Publication Data

Shaffer, Bev, 1951-
  Cookies to die for! / Bev Shaffer ; food photography and food styling by John R.
Shaffer.
      p. cm.
  Includes bibliographical references and index.
  ISBN 978-1-58980-610-8 (hbk. : alk. paper) 1. Cookies. I. Title.
TX772.S49 2009
641.8'654—dc22
                                2008034679

Printed in China
Published by Pelican Publishing Company, Inc.
1000 Burmaster Street, Gretna, Louisiana 70053

Just when you think you have more time than necessary, life happens. That being said, I am grateful to a very large handful of people for their assistance with this labor of cookie love.

To my husband and dear friend, John, for his recipe testing, food styling, food photography, overall support, coordinating cookie testers, and making dinner. He's the kind of man to whom I can say, "You know, I really don't like that cookie photo at all," and he'll say, "Okay, we'll change it." (Now, he may go upstairs to his office and grumble, but I never know it!) I convinced him a few years ago to move from nature photography to food photography, and his food photos just keep getting mouthwateringly better. I guess I have to face it; he's just the perfect guy!

Special thanks to my friend, Vickie Getz, for unflinchingly reading and proofing the manuscript throughout the process. (Sorry we went down to the twelfth hour on this one, Vick!)

My cookie testers, oh, you sweet bakers. Special thanks to these ladies who each agreed to test a series of recipes on their own time, write baking notes, make comments, and gain a few pounds along with us. My sincere appreciation to: Julianna Baillis, Paula Horvath, Lisa Maglionico, Lisa Dellafiora, Tammy Bradfield, Barbara Cumming, Annette Felton, and Annette Sarich.

Fancifully decorating cookies is just not my thing, so special thanks also goes to Annette Felton for her crafting of the images of gingerbread cutouts, decorated cookies, and the flowerpot cookies.

Warm thanks to everyone at Pelican Publishing Company—from the warehouse staff to the office staff to the production and graphics department—for embracing this (and my other cookbooks) and then lavishing it with extraordinary attention. In particular, my appreciation goes to: Milburn and Nancy Calhoun, for their hospitality and support; Nina Kooij and the editorial staff; Kathleen Calhoun Nettleton and the promotion department; and Joseph Billingsley and the sales department.

Two manufacturers provided me with equipment I especially appreciated. I had fun using Chef's Choice PizzellePro Express Bake 835, which was perfectly sized for entertaining (and I am not easily entertained). It made three pizzelles every 45 to 60 seconds. My cookie sheets went through more uses than most of our cookie sheets go through in a lifetime. Anolon provided me with several of their cookie sheets (both nonstick and regular), and my favorites were the Anolon Commercial Bakeware, in particular the 14x16" size. These extremely sturdy sheets gave me even browning, resisted warping in the oven, and were easy to clean.

More than one of my testers told me they hadn't made cookies in awhile and I had inspired them to bake again. My hope is a cookie or two will inspire *you* to take the time to know what goes into these simple, everyday pleasures. Handcraft several cookies over several weeks, only then can you choose whether to share them with friends and family . . . or horde them for yourself!

CONTENTS

Just one bite of these Gingerbread Streusel Thins will confirm that you can never be too thin—or have too much streusel!!

COOKIE BITES

Growing up in a very ethnic family (Hungarian mother, Italian father) there was always something cooking and baking, and cookies are a big part of those memories.

I don't recall standing around the kitchen counter in my pinafore apron, taking my sweet old time decorating cute little cut-out cookies like so many of my Americanized friends did. We were into production, and when I think back, it was, of course, all done with a mixing bowl and a wooden spoon. No electric mixers, no food processors . . . the only thing that plugged in was the oven. It was all lovingly handmade.

So what were these cookie traditions? Kiflis, those gems of the Hungarian world that are made with a cream-cheese dough and are flaky and truly irresistible when warm . . . so irresistible you forget you're eating them until you notice the huge voids on the cooling racks where cookies used to be.

My mom was a true traditionalist when it came to baking those heritage recipes. She and her sisters grew up with fillings made of freshly ground poppy seeds, cooked in milk and butter, sweetened with sugar, and lightened by the flavor of lemon zest. No zester grater for these women; it was a box grater (I remember the handle was coming off the one in my childhood kitchen), and I don't remember the word "pith" ever being mentioned. These women just knew how to get the zest, and the zest only, off the lemon. There were fillings made of egg whites, whipped with a whisk to stiff peaks and folded into freshly ground walnuts (lots of them, pounds of them, not this 1 cup stuff we know today), with sugar and, once again, lemon zest to intensify the flavor. And, of course, there was the lekvar (prune butter) filling, which was the *only* filling my mom and aunts purchased. (Need I tell you it was imported from Hungary?)

But in our kitchen, there was NEVER apricot filling, so that delectable treat was satisfied, at holiday time only, when I visited a friend of German descent. Her mom made their version of kiflis with an apricot filling, and I tried, often times unsuccessfully, not to make a pig of myself.

We rolled, shaped, filled, and baked so many kiflis during Christmas and Easter that I often thought we were feeding all of New Jersey. But alas, soon they were gone until holiday time came around again.

During Christmas, we made Press Cookies. Huge batches of round, pressed cookies topped with glacé cherry halves. I would often eat the cherry half off *before* they went in the oven, but my help was too valuable, and I was never chased out of the kitchen for such behavior. (My Mom would just give me *the look* and I would stop.) We'd make green tree-shaped dough, press it out, and top it with colorful sprinkles. It was a sturdy cookie press with a comfortable handle and a barrel that held a substantial amount of dough. I still have that cookie press.

And that was it—no chocolate chip cookies, no oatmeal cookies when the holidays were not upon us. Since those formative years, I've been baking lots of cookies—rolled and sliced cookies, bar cookies, shaped and pressed cookies, cut-out cookies, and scooped and dropped cookies. Think of a combination of flavors and textures and I have—more than likely—taught it, demonstrated it, reworked it, gifted it, or made it and filed it away in my cookie collection memory bank. So, cookies to me, just as seasonal foods are touted today, bring anticipation of great flavors and wonderful memories in the kitchen.

This book invites you to start your own baking traditions at your home, although I highly recommend you bake cookies more than twice a year! There are some easy, flavorful recipes in this book you can put together in no time; some that are a little more complicated, and many that will become favorites—cookies you'll treat your friends, family, and yourself to again and again.

So, gather up that Organic Valley unsalted butter, that Bob's Red Mill unbleached white flour (my preferences, without apologies), the finest granulated cane sugar, chocolate and spices, and whatever else you need, and yes, pull out the stand mixer and plug it in. Heat the oven—I have my apron ready. Let's bake together and enjoy some great cookies my mom and aunts would be proud of!

COOKIES
to die for!

*A basketful of sweet goodness . . . an assortment of
cookies to die for!*

COOKIE BASICS

From dough to decorations, baking to freezing, these sweet secrets will help ensure delicious cookie results. Now is the time to get out the mixing bowls, electric mixer, baking sheets, and wire cooling racks. Filling your cookie jar with crisp, chewy, or gooey goodies has never been easier.

My ingredients mostly include butter (I prefer unsalted and organic for that sweet, pure butter flavor), granulated pure cane sugar, large eggs (brown shell, organic), and unbleached, all-purpose flour (organic, but the most critical element is the unbleached). Use real butter, not margarine; margarine contains some water and will alter the texture of cookies and make for a less desirable flavor.

The recipes in this book call for various sugars: confectioners' sugar (always sift before use) dissolves easily, granulated sugar creates crunch and adds bulk, and brown sugar (light or dark, always firmly pack when measuring) contributes moisture to a cookie and a natural caramel flavor.

Measure precisely! Baking is a science and accuracy in measuring is important. When the recipe calls for softened (room temperature) butter, it should yield slightly to pressure yet not lose its shape when touched.

Don't overmix the dough once the dry ingredients are added; doing so often times results in one tough cookie (an admirable thing in a person, not a baked treat!) or a cookie that simply doesn't rise to the occasion. So, what's a baker to do? Mix just until the ingredients are combined, stopping to scrape the bowl often. I prefer a stand mixer for cookie dough; it allows me to easily combine ingredients and whip in air for a lighter texture.

When it comes to cookie sheets, I prefer heavy, shiny metal flat pans, with a lip on only one side. Cookies baked on nonstick sheets and dark cookie sheets have a tendency to brown too much on the bottom. Unless you're baking bar cookies, I prefer not to bake cookies on rimmed jellyroll pans, as they deflect heat and capture excess moisture, which makes for one soggy cookie! Parchment paper is still my preferred means of lining cookie sheets (even though I own silicone liners). Lining your sheets in this way, as opposed to greasing or spraying, keeps the sheets looking like new and prevents grease build up. I bake my bar cookies in shiny metal pans or good-quality ceramic pans, as opposed to glass. Glass conducts the heat differently, and I have found inconsistent results. Your oven should be heated to the proper temperature before you begin baking. Invest in an oven thermometer for accuracy each and every time.

Wire cooling racks are a must, and I prefer the very large size with a grid pattern (so the delicate, small cookies don't fall through). These racks allow air to circulate under the cookies as they cool, keeping them from becoming soggy. For doughs that are chilled before baking, this helps solidify the fat and keeps the cookies from overspreading when they bake. Also, be sure to place your dough on cool baking sheets, as warm or hot pans will cause the cookies to spread or puff too much. You can quickly cool a baking sheet by placing it under cold running water; dry it thoroughly before arranging dough on the pan.

Always allow some room for spreading so cookies don't bake together into one huge amoeba (refer to fifth-grade science). I like to bake cookies in the middle of the oven or on the second rack from the bottom. If you bake two cookie sheets at once, which you almost always will do, rotate them halfway through the baking time. I rotate the pans top to bottom and front to back to ensure a more even bake. Allow your baked cookies to remain on the sheets for a few minutes before transferring them to wire cooling racks. If you try to remove them too soon, it usually results in broken cookies. (A fiendish trick if you want to try a not-so-perfect one in a hurry.)

SWEET SECRETS: INGREDIENTS

As I've mentioned, I naturally have ingredient preferences that I feel work best when creating and baking off recipes.

When it comes to flour, your best bet for general baking is an all-purpose flour, and an unbleached version (bleaching chemically whitens the flour) is my overall choice. To measure flour, spoon it into your measuring cup and use the flat side of a knife to level it.

When a recipe calls for eggs, always use large-size eggs unless otherwise specified. Crack the eggs into a small bowl before adding to the other ingredients; this way you can remove any stray pieces of shell that may have fallen into the bowl.

For superior flavor and texture you simply can't beat butter (well, you can beat it but only when it's softened). To soften butter, leave at room temperature for 30 minutes (cutting it into small pieces speeds up the process).

Baking soda and baking powder are not interchangeable. Baking soda works when mixed with an acidic ingredient such as buttermilk, sour cream, or vinegar. On the other hand, baking powder works with a neutral liquid, such as water or milk, to cause rising.

I would be remiss if I didn't mention chocolate. Even for everyday baking, buy the best-quality chocolate (remember, your final product is only as good as the ingredients you've used). Most often, I use semisweet or unsweetened chocolate, or an unsweetened cocoa powder. If you prefer, as I often do, a bolder chocolate taste, choose bittersweet. Remember that bittersweet and semisweet are interchangeable, depending on what degree of sweetness you like your chocolate. Bittersweet contains less sugar than semisweet chocolate.

SWEET SECRETS: BAKING TIPS

From general hints to the top baking tips, this information will help you enjoy baking bliss.

Read through each recipe and assemble ingredients (chefs refer to this as *mise en place* or all things in their place). Prep ahead. Be sure you have the proper utensils and pan sizes needed as well.

Measure dry and liquid ingredients accurately to prevent your cookies and bars from becoming dry and crumbly or so soft that they spread out of shape during baking. Baking is a science, so measure up!

Heat your oven for 10 to 15 minutes before you begin baking. The oven and its gauge may not always agree, so use an oven thermometer. Keep in mind that the oven temperature drops 25 degrees every time the oven door is opened.

Lighten up a little. Don't overmix or beat the dough vigorously after adding the flour, or your baked goods may become tough.

For bar cookies, be sure to use the correct pan size. Center your baking pan or sheet in a preheated oven for optimum heat circulation.

Watch baking time carefully. If two sheets are in the oven at the same time, switch their positions midway through baking, helping to ensure more uniform results.

Cool cookies on wire cooling racks to ensure even air circulation. Hot cookie sheets need to cool, too; this helps prevent your cookies from spreading unnecessarily.

A few more things:

Use the freshest ingredients possible. The butter should be very fresh (considering that much of the flavor of a cookie is from the quality of this ingredient). Spices, nuts, and dried fruits should all be fresh, not old, shriveled, and flavorless.

The right touch (butter at the right consistency) is important to make sure that your cookies don't spread too much or not enough. Softened butter should give just slightly and leave an indentation when pressed down with a finger, while melted butter should be fluid and translucent. If you are in a hurry, cut the butter into tablespoon-sized pieces to speed softening; it will be soft enough to use in about 15 minutes.

Resist substituting with light or diet tub margarines or spreads as these contain not only less fat but more water and can cause a multitude of problems. The type of fat used in a recipe will affect results.

Remember that cookies will continue to bake on hot pans after they are removed from the oven. To avoid overbaking, remove the sheets from the oven a minute or two before cookies are completely done and browned to your liking. If you want an oatmeal cookie, for example, that's chewy in the middle, take them out of the oven before they look done. The cookies will set up as they cool.

SWEET SECRETS: COMMON COOKING MEASURES

These handy charts will help with the most common of questions, such as what exactly does a ½ cup of butter equal?

ABBREVIATIONS

STANDARD

tsp.	=	teaspoon
tbsp.	=	tablespoon
oz.	=	ounce
qt.	=	quart
lb.	=	pound

METRIC

ml.	=	milliliter
l.	=	liter
g.	=	gram
kg.	=	kilogram
mg.	=	milligram

MEASURE CONVERSION TABLE

1 teaspoon	=	$\frac{1}{3}$ tablespoon
3 teaspoons	=	1 tablespoon
2 tablespoons	=	$\frac{1}{8}$ cup
4 tablespoons	=	$\frac{1}{4}$ cup
8 tablespoons	=	$\frac{1}{2}$ cup
12 tablespoons	=	$\frac{3}{4}$ cup
14 tablespoons	=	$\frac{7}{8}$ cup
16 tablespoons	=	1 cup
1 pint	=	2 cups
1 quart	=	2 pints
1 liter	=	1.057 quarts
1 gram	=	0.35 ounces
1 ounce	=	28.35 grams
1 pound	=	16 ounces

STANDARD-METRIC APPROXIMATIONS

$\frac{1}{8}$ teaspoon	=			.6 milliliter
$\frac{1}{4}$ teaspoon	=			1.2 milliliters
$\frac{1}{2}$ teaspoon	=			2.5 milliliters
1 teaspoon	=			5 milliliters
1 tablespoon	=			15 milliliters
4 tablespoons	=	$\frac{1}{4}$ cup	=	60 milliliters
8 tablespoons	=	$\frac{1}{2}$ cup	=	118 milliliters
16 tablespoons	=	1 cup	=	236 milliliters
2 cups			=	473 milliliters
$2\frac{1}{2}$ cups			=	563 milliliters
4 cups			=	946 milliliters
1 quart	=	4 cups	=	.94 liter

SOLID MEASUREMENTS

$\frac{1}{2}$ ounce			=	15 grams
1 ounce			=	25 grams
4 ounces			=	110 grams
16 ounces	=	1 pound	=	454 grams

Cookie baking "must haves" include a kitchen scale, zesters, sieves, oven thermometer, heavy cookie sheets, parchment paper, and several spatulas.

SWEET SECRETS: GET EQUIPPED

For batch after batch of delicious cookies, follow my basic cookie sheet secrets:

* Use light-colored, heavy cookie sheets for best results. Dark sheets may cause cookies to overbrown. If you must use darker sheets, bake cookies for 1 to 2 minutes less. Do not use baking pans with high sides.

* Use cookie sheets that are at least 2 inches narrower and shorter than the oven.

* Always let cookie sheets cool before placing dough on them. Hot cookie sheets may cause cookies to spread and brown too much.

Having the right equipment is essential to great baking. Here's what I love to have on hand.

A spring-handled cookie scoop, portion-control scoop, or disher are a baker's best friend. They produce perfectly uniform, in size and shape, scoop and drop cookies. But what are those numbers engraved on the handles? Usually the number of the scoop indicates the number of level scoopfuls it takes to make 1 quart. The following gives an approximate measure for each scoop:

More baking necessities to make life easier: rolling pin, flour shaker, dough scraper, pastry brushes, measuring cups, measuring spoons, large cloth-covered board (for rolling dough)

Scoop Number 100	=	2 teaspoons
Scoop Number 70	=	$2^3/_4$ teaspoons
Scoop Number 60	=	$3^1/_4$ teaspoons
Scoop Number 50	=	$3^3/_4$ teaspoons
Scoop Number 40	=	$1^2/_3$ tablespoons
Scoop Number 30	=	2 tablespoons
Scoop Number 24	=	$2^3/_4$ tablespoons
Scoop Number 20	=	$3^1/_3$ tablespoons
Scoop Number 16	=	$^1/_4$ cup
Scoop Number 12	=	$^1/_3$ cup

It's Just Grate: originally designed to function as a woodworking tool, a Microplane® grater-zester is a kitchen gadget tailor made for grating citrus zest. This tool makes it a breeze. I adore how its razor-sharp edges shave off the zest effortlessly. To use this tool, or a traditional lemon zester that pulls off the rind in thin strips, first wash and dry the fruit. Then, working over a piece of wax paper, rub the fruit over the grating holes with quick strokes. Don't apply too much pressure; the white pith is bitter. Strips from a traditional zester will need to be finely chopped before using.

Remember that not all measuring cups are created equal. Use flat-topped cups for dry ingredients, such as flour, and glass or plastic cups, with a spout for pouring and increments on the side, to measure liquids.

Parchment paper or silicone baking mats are perfect to line your baking sheets. There's no need for greasing your pans and cleanup will be a breeze.

Rolling dough for cut-out cookies is an easy task with my favorite piece of baking equipment, a round board (19") with rubber feet to prevent slipping. It has a removable cloth cover for washing. And I always use my tapered rolling pin, no ball bearings necessary.

As Mae West once said, "too much of a good thing is wonderful." Thus, I share here with you, just for the fun of it, my cookie-cutter collection, which is mostly metal. Note that not every cutter was used to test recipes in this book!

Bev's available cookie-cutter collection includes: house with chimney; various and assorted sizes of circles; various and assorted sizes of hearts; mini teddy bear; mini apples; various and assorted sizes of Christmas trees; mini holly; a very large State of Texas (is anything small about Texas?!); large maple leaf; plastic turtle; large white plastic numbers 1, 2, 3, 4, 5, 6, 7, 8, 0; plastic camel; plastic teddy bear; plastic dove; plastic bunny; large reclining cat; dog bone; large heart with arrow; ice cream cone; library symbol (person and book); medium duck; pear; large, copper State of Ohio (unfortunately not as large as Texas!); large, copper pineapple; medium, copper whale; plastic acorn; elephant; biscuit cutter (round/reversible—plain and scalloped); duck; cat; bat; teapot; dinosaurs (assorted); toothbrush; pumpkin; musical note; anchor; donkey; star; man in the moon (crescent); lips, two sizes; umbrella; hand; running gingerbread man; crinkled star; medium heart with arrow; train engine car (or John thinks that this one is a running squirrel!); angel; Santa (assorted types); medium bell; medium piggy; turkey; mini bunny head; mini gingerbread girl; mini gingerbread boys (2); mini star; mini butterfly; mini bunny; mini reindeer; a set of graduated-size crinkle oval cutters; a set of graduated-size crinkled rounds; a set of graduated-size plain rounds; diamond; bunny; very large turkey; brontosaurus; crinkle fan; g-man; cardinal; 6½-inch queen; foot; shamrock; tooth; leaf; turtle; teddy bear; apple; medium State of Ohio; pineapple; airplane; papa bear; elephant; medium bunny; cowboy boot; g-man (with handle); g-man (large); baby buggy; mini pumpkin; mini baby chick; arrow; umbrella; rolling pin; egg; angel; daisy; fireplug; shooting star; large cowboy hat; cactus; palm tree; small gingerbread boy; jalapeño pepper; mini cactus; mini star; mini airplane; mini cross; mini birdhouse; mini carrot; mini leaf; mini egg; witch hat; large bat; ghost; reindeer; scaredy cat; 4½" copper g-man; large star; tiered (wedding) cake; high-heel shoe; gingerbread house; large butterfly; large palm tree; snowflake set (3 shapes). Whew!

SWEET SECRETS: ARE YOU MY TYPE?

The following are some special helps for specific cookie types, with more information appearing in each recipe's instructions.

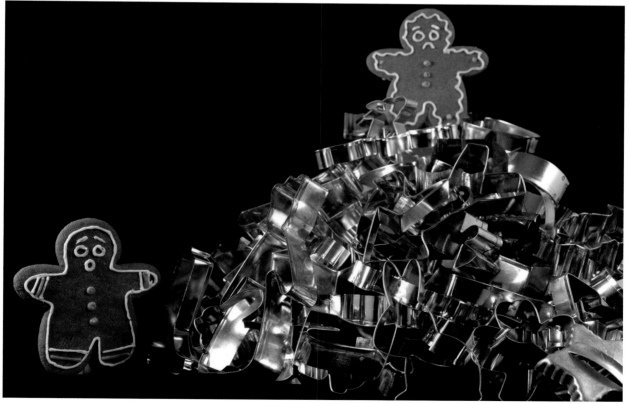

You found your way up there, now find your way down!

Bars: For best appearance, cool in pan completely before cutting into pieces unless otherwise stated in recipe. Some do and some don't like to use the "foil release" method for bar cookies. If you do, line the pan completely with foil (being sure the foil doesn't tear and does overhang at least 1" above the pan's edges). Gently grease the foil (if called for in the recipe). When the bars are completely cooled, this method enables you to carefully lift the entire "bar" out of the pan, fold down the foil, then cut without pan interference.

Drop: For uniform-sized cookies, use the same amount of dough for each cookie and mound each slightly. For ease in achieving this, a scale, 2 regular teaspoons, or a commercially made cookie-dough disher, dropper, or scoop work well.

Shaped: It is often times beneficial to chill dough for easier handling, dusting hands lightly with flour to help prevent sticking when rolling each cookie smoothly between palms of hands. For "flattened" cookies, press each scoop of dough with a fork, bottom of a glass dipped in sugar or flour, or a thumb. To maximize flavor and appearance, cookies to be rolled in confectioners' sugar or cocoa powder should be coated once while still warm and then again after cooling.

Pressed: For tender cookies, use room temperature butter, creaming with other ingredients just until light and fluffy. Test consistency by pushing a small amount of dough through the press. Dough that is too soft may benefit from a brief period of refrigeration or the addition of 1 to 2 tablespoons of flour. Dough that is too stiff may be remedied with the addition of a tablespoon of milk or 1 egg yolk. Beginning with a cool baking sheet, hold press so it rests on sheet and force dough onto sheet, raising press only when correct form is achieved.

Refrigerator: For firm, smoothly shaped rolls, wrap rolls of dough securely in plastic wrap or waxed paper and chill for 30 minutes. Remove and roll back and forth on counter until a cylindrical shape is reached. Refrigerate, tightly wrapped, for at least 2 hours up to overnight to allow roll to firm up completely. Unwrap and slice evenly with a thin, sharp knife for baking.

Rolled: For tender cookies, roll out small amounts of dough from center to edges with light, even strokes. A floured pastry cloth and lightly floured rolling pin are helpful to roll out dough with a minimum of flour on the rolling surface. I always use a rolling-the-dough flour mixture of $\frac{2}{3}$-part flour and $\frac{1}{3}$-part confectioners' sugar, sifted, for a light, flavorful cookie. For a crisper cookie, roll thinly; for a softer cookie, roll thicker. Cut cookies as closely together as possible using cutters dipped in flour. To prevent breaking, move cookies to and from baking sheets with a wide spatula or pancake turner.

SWEET SECRETS: ANY WAY YOU SPREAD 'EM

Icing, frosting, or glaze, no matter what you call 'em, these pleasurable toppings might very well be the icing on your next cookie!

Royal Icing

This icing hardens as it dries and is ideal for piping decorations on cooled cookies.

1¼ cups confectioners' sugar, sifted
1 tbsp. meringue powder
2 tbsp. warm water
¼ tsp. cream of tartar

Combine the confectioners' sugar, meringue powder, warm water, and cream of tartar in a large mixing bowl. Beat at low speed with an electric mixer until moistened. Increase the speed to medium. Beat until stiff and glossy (2 to 4 minutes). Add an additional tbsp. of hot water if too stiff.

Cover bowl with a damp towel until ready to use or cover with plastic wrap and refrigerate for 1 day. To restore texture, allow icing to reach room temperature, then rebeat. Makes about ¾ cup.

Best Buttercream Frosting

This is a creamy butter frosting, a perfect base for a variety of flavored frostings as well.

¾ cup unsalted butter, softened
6 cups confectioners' sugar, sifted
⅛ tsp. salt
⅓ cup heavy (whipping) cream
1 tsp. vanilla
2 tbsp. light corn syrup

Place butter in a large mixer bowl. Beat at medium speed with an electric mixer, scraping bowl occasionally, until creamy (about 2 minutes).

Gradually add confectioners' sugar and salt, alternately with heavy cream and vanilla, scraping bowl often, until well blended. Beat in corn syrup until well mixed. Makes about 3 cups.

Two to three cups of frosting is enough to decorate at least 2 to 3 dozen cookies.

Best Buttercream Variations

Variety is the frosting of life!

Lemon/Orange Frosting: Stir in 1 tbsp. of freshly grated and finely chopped lemon or orange zest.

Creamy Coconut Frosting: Stir in 1½ tsp. of coconut extract.

Chocolate Frosting: Add 1 or 2 oz. of unsweetened chocolate, melted and cooled; an additional tbsp. or two of sifted confectioners' sugar may be necessary to reach the desired spreading consistency.

Creamy Butter Frosting

This creamy frosting is great for decorating. Tint with food coloring if desired.

4 cups confectioners' sugar, sifted
½ cup unsalted butter, softened
2 tbsp. vanilla
3 to 4 tbsp. milk, whole or 2 percent

Combine the confectioners' sugar, butter, and vanilla in a small mixer bowl. Beat at low speed with an electric mixer, gradually adding milk and scraping the bowl often, until you have reached the desired spreading consistency.

Decorate cooled cookies or bars. Cover; store refrigerated. Makes 2¼ cups.

Confectioners' Sugar Glaze

This glaze hardens on standing and gives cookies the perfect glazed surface for decorating. Tint with food coloring if desired.

2½ cups confectioners' sugar, sifted
2 tbsp. water
1 tbsp. unsalted butter, softened
1 tbsp. light corn syrup
½ tsp. vanilla or almond extract, if desired

Combine the confectioners' sugar, water, butter, corn syrup, and vanilla in a small mixer bowl. Beat at medium speed with an electric mixer until smooth, adding additional water if necessary to achieve desired spreading consistency.

Glaze cookies. Let stand until hardened (6 hours or overnight). Makes 1 cup.

SWEET SECRETS: STORAGE STRATEGIES

In General:
   Store baked cookies only after they're completely cooled. Condensation makes them soggy if stored while they're still warm. Cooled cookies are best stored in an airtight container if the cookies are crisp, in a loosely covered container if the cookies are soft. Cookie jar storage is for short-term keeping only.

Store Me or Freeze Me:
   Store crisp and softer cookies separately. Softer cookies will leach moisture (oh my!) that will cause crisp cookies to go limp. If crisp cookies do soften, you can recrisp them by baking at 300 degrees for 5 minutes, then cooling completely on a wire rack. To soften up stale cookies, add a piece of apple to the container, discarding it after 1 day.

Bar cookies may be stored, tightly covered, in the baking pan. For food safety, some frostings, fillings, or other ingredients may require refrigerator storage. I don't recommend freezing unbaked bar cookies. If you can live without the pan for awhile, you can freeze cooled bars right in the baking pan, with plastic wrap pressed directly on the surface; cover the whole pan tightly with foil.

Frosted or filled thumbprint cookies should be stored in a single layer in a tightly covered container. If space is limited, allow frosting or filling to become firm before storing, then layer cookies between waxed paper to protect appearance.

Most cookie doughs can be refrigerated for up to 2 days (tightly wrapped in plastic wrap and foil or stored in an airtight container to prevent the dough from drying out or picking up odors from other foods) or frozen for up to 3 months in an airtight container or freezer bag. (Dough will need to be thawed in the refrigerator about 8 hours before using). If the dough is frozen in cookie "portions," there's no need to thaw the frozen dough, just bake an additional 1 or 2 minutes.

Rolled and cut-out cookies (unbaked and decorated or simply cut out and left plain until later) should be stored between layers of waxed paper in the freezer for up to 3 months.

Slice and bake cookies are a breeze to freeze. Freeze the dough logs, and then slice just before baking. If the dough logs are too firm, thaw just slightly at room temperature for 10 to 15 minutes. Logs freeze well for up to 3 months.

Except for meringues, scooped and dropped cookies can be frozen in dough balls in a single layer on a baking sheet, then transferred to a heavy-duty Ziploc plastic storage bag and stored in the freezer for up to 3 months. Before final shaping, thaw slightly at room temperature for 10 to 15 minutes.

At holiday time, you may wind up with lots of baked cookies. Here's an overview of the best way to freeze them (but I can't guarantee that a certain someone won't raid your freezer and eat them all!):

* Remember to separate the cookies by type (crispy or chewy).
* Cookies and bars are easier to stack and freeze without the frosting or glaze. You can always plan to add the frosting or glaze to thawed cookies and bars.
* Store cookies in freezer containers, between layers of wax paper.
* Seal containers tightly, label, and date.
* Thaw cookies in the original containers at room temperature so that condensation forms on the wrapping, not on the cookies! Or, for crisp cookies, unwrap them and place in a single layer on a plate for about 15 minutes. This will prevent them from becoming soggy.

SWEET SECRETS: THAT SHOULDN'T BE THE WAY THE COOKIE CRUMBLES

Below are some possible problems, potential causes, and suggested fixes—sweet secrets indeed!

Cookie Problem: Spreading/Flat
Potential Causes and Suggested Fixes:

Dough was placed on hot/warm cookie sheets. Let cookie sheets cool between uses.

Low oven temperature. Use an oven thermometer to check actual temperature and adjust accordingly. Be sure to preheat the oven 10 to 15 minutes before baking. A good habit is to turn the oven on as the first step of the recipe.

Greased cookie sheet. Only grease or line cookie sheet if recipe directs.

Old Fashioned/Rolled Oats absorb water slower than Quick Oats. Refrigerate cookie dough 20 minutes, or until firm. Cookies will take slightly longer to bake completely.

Warm kitchen causes dough to become very soft. Refrigerate cookie dough 20 minutes, or until firm. Cookies will take slightly longer to bake completely.

Cookie Problem: Doughy
Potential Causes and Suggested Fixes:

Cookies are underbaked. Do not use cookie sheets that have sides that prevent hot air from circulating around the cookies.

Insulated cookie sheets don't get as hot as a regular cookie sheet. Bake cookies longer than the suggested time range since most recipes are not developed for insulated cookie sheet use.

Cookies are not uniform in size, which means they don't bake evenly. Use 2 teaspoons, a measuring tablespoon, a commercial cookie disher, or scoop to portion out cookie dough and ensure that all are a similar size.

Cookie Problem: Soggy/Crumbly
Potential Causes and Suggested Fixes:

Cookies cooled on sheet too long. Follow cooling directions in recipe. If no directions are given, immediately remove cookies from sheet and place on a wire rack in a single layer to cool completely.

Cookies placed in storage container while still warm. Cool cookies completely on a wire rack before putting in a storage container.

Cookie Problem: Dry/Hard as rocks

Potential Causes and Suggested Fixes:

Using shortening in a recipe that calls for butter. When using shortening in a recipe that calls for butter, it is necessary to add some additional water or milk. Add 1 tablespoon for each ½ cup shortening. Example: for 1 cup shortening, add 2 tablespoons water.

Overmixed dough. Don't vigorously mix the dry ingredients into the wet ingredients. Overmixing is easy to do with electric mixers.

Overmeasuring dry ingredients. Spoon dry ingredients into measuring cups; don't scoop.

Cookie Problem: Difficult to remove from sheet

Potential Causes and Suggested Fixes:

Often lower fat cookies will stick to the sheet. Line cookie sheet with parchment paper, silicone liner, or spray cookie sheet with nonstick vegetable oil cooking spray.

Cookies cooled on sheet too long. Follow cooling directions in recipe. If no directions are given, immediately remove cookies from sheet and place on a wire rack in a single layer to cool completely. Return sheet of cookies to hot oven for 1 minute, then loosen cookies and remove to wire rack to cool.

Cookie Problem: Dark/Burned

Potential Causes and Suggested Fixes:

You're not paying attention. Set timer.

Using a dark-colored cookie sheet. Use a light-colored cookie sheet, which doesn't get as hot as a dark-colored sheet because it absorbs less heat. This helps prevent cookies from overbrowning.

Oven rack too low. Place rack in the center of the oven.

Oven temperature too high. Use an oven thermometer to check the actual oven temperature and adjust accordingly.

Cookies placed close to the edge of the sheet will bake faster than cookies in the center. Avoid jamming as many cookies as possible onto a sheet. Instead, place cookies about 2 inches apart and avoid putting them close to the edge.

Cookie sheet is too big for the oven, preventing hot air from circulating around the sheet. Use a cookie sheet that is at least 2 inches smaller than the oven so that the warm air will circulate evenly around the sheet.

SWEET SECRETS: SHARING

Sharing your cookies with a roomful of friends is one of life's sweet joys. The cookie exchange is ever popular, with the tradition of having guests bring a batch (or more) of one kind (or more) of cookie to an exchange party, where they can swap and take home an assortment, has spread to every corner of the country.

The perfect opportunity to spend a relaxing afternoon with friends and return home with a variety of cookies you didn't have to bake yourself is a wonderful idea. Never hosted a cookie exchange? The following are some tips for hosting a perfectly sweet party of your own:

* Invite no more than twelve people. Ask each guest to bake and bring three or four dozen cookies of one kind (or more for the ambitious).

* Remember that the cookies are the guests of honor and should be featured prominently. A cookie exchange is the perfect time to pull out your favorite decorative plates, tiered cake stands, doilies, vintage tablecloths, or anything to make the cookies even more inviting.

* At the party, guests will package and take home a selection of every type of cookie except their own—just be sure that everyone knows the limit so that all of the attendees end up with approximately the same number of cookies.

* Holiday cookies are always a crowd pleaser, but there's nothing wrong with having your guests bring a childhood favorite cookie. Have a "favorite cookie" contest, giving everyone a chance to vote, and awarding a copy of this book, **COOKIES to Die For!**, as the prize.

* Don't forget to provide light appetizers and refreshing drinks, and some tins or boxes and waxed paper for everyone to pack up their favorites at the end.

SWEET SECRETS: COOKIES GO BYE-BYE

Packing Tips for Shipping Cookies:

The best cookies for mailing are soft, moist, and sturdy, such as oatmeal cookies or some bar cookies.

Avoid mailing cookies that are thin, fragile, frosted, or have pointed edges that may break off. (Instead, eat them immediately!)

Remember to keep soft and crisp cookies separate.

To pack the cookies, select a sturdy box and line it with waxed paper or plastic wrap, then cushion the bottom with crumpled newspaper. Pack the cookies in one of two ways:

* This Way—Pack the cookies in tins or coffee cans, separating layers with waxed paper. Heavy cookies should be in the bottom layers. Then place the tins in the lined box, surrounding sides and top with more crumpled newspaper before sealing.

* That Way—If containers are not used, wrap cookies in pairs (back to back), or wrap bar cookies individually with plastic wrap or foil. Pack them in a lined box so they don't shift around. Top with another layer of crumpled newspaper before sealing.

ROLLED AND CUT AND SHAPED
AND PRESSED COOKIES

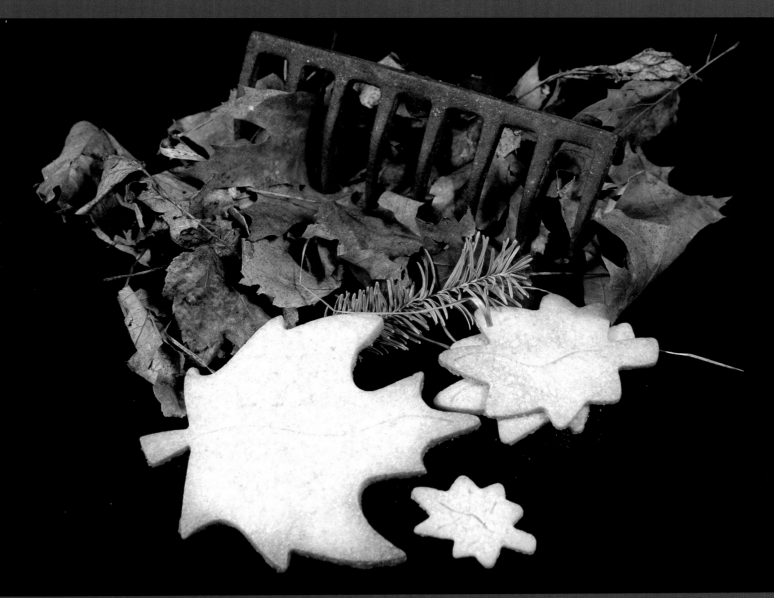

*Raking becomes more of a treat than a chore when there are
Maple Butter Cookies to "clean up."*

Rolled and Cut

Did you know?

Dipping cookie cutters into flour or confectioners' sugar helps make clean cuts and prevents them from sticking to the dough.

You should start cutting from the outside edge and work your way across, keeping the dough intact until you've cut all the shapes into it, then peel back the scraps.

After you've gently rerolled the scraps, only cut one more batch. The dough will be overworked, resulting in a tough cookie, if they're rerolled more than once.

If you want those cut outs to retain their original shapes, be sure the dough and pan are cold as they go into the oven to bake.

Shaped and Pressed

Great fun for your hands:

Dough will be less likely to stick to your warm hands if you dust them with confectioners' sugar or lightly grease them with oil or cooking spray before handling the dough.

Having trouble with those thumbprint indentations holding their shape? Chill the dough thoroughly after making the thumbprint indentations, then bake as directed.

Patience, please. Spoon your filling into those baked thumbprint cookies only after they're completely cool.

Ginger Babies

A crisp, sugary flavorful ginger cookie perfect with a hot cup of your favorite tea!

2 cups granulated sugar
1½ cups unsalted butter, room
    temperature
½ cup molasses
2 large eggs
4½ cups unbleached, all-purpose flour
1 tbsp. baking soda
½ tsp. salt
2 tsp. ground cinnamon
1 tsp. ground cloves
1 tsp. ground ginger
½ tsp. freshly grated nutmeg
Demerara sugar or additional granulated
    sugar for rolling

BEV'S BITES

I prefer the milder flavor of Barbados molasses, but Blackstrap molasses will work just as well in this recipe.

Using an electric mixer, in a large bowl, beat together the sugar, butter, molasses, and eggs until light and fluffy.

In a small bowl, blend together the flour, baking soda, salt, cinnamon, cloves, ginger, and nutmeg; mix well. Add to the mixing bowl, blending to combine.

Cover with plastic wrap; refrigerate for 1 to 2 hours.

Heat oven to 350 degrees. Shape dough into 1" balls; roll in additional sugar until coated. Place 1" apart on ungreased cookie sheets. During baking, these cookies will puff up then flatten.

Bake for 9 to 12 minutes or until set. Cool 1 minute, then remove from cookie sheets to wire racks to cool completely. Makes about 9 dozen.

Green Tea Ruffles

A pairing of orange and green tea make for a delicate cookie with an unusual flavor combination.

3 cups unbleached, all-purpose flour
1 cup granulated sugar
2 tsp. green tea leaves, finely ground
1 tsp. baking powder
$\frac{1}{2}$ tsp. baking soda
1 cup unsalted butter, room temperature
$\frac{1}{3}$ cup orange juice
1 tbsp. fresh orange zest, finely grated

GLAZE

$\frac{1}{4}$ cup granulated sugar
$\frac{1}{4}$ cup freshly brewed green tea
2 tbsp. honey

Using an electric mixer, in a large bowl, combine the flour, sugar, ground green tea, baking powder, baking soda, butter, orange juice, and zest. Blend well, stopping to scrape down the sides of the bowl, until mixture is combined.

Cover bowl with plastic wrap and refrigerate for 30 minutes.

Heat oven to 400 degrees.

Roll dough out onto a lightly floured surface to $\frac{1}{8}$" thick. Cut with oval, ruffle-shaped cookie cutters, or other shapes as desired. Place on ungreased cookie sheets.

Bake for 6 to 8 minutes or until a light golden brown on top. Cool 1 minute, then remove from cookie sheets to wire racks to cool completely.

For the Glaze: In a small saucepan, combine the sugar, brewed green tea, and honey. Bring to a boil, then reduce heat and simmer for 5 minutes. Allow Glaze to cool just enough so it doesn't burn your fingers, then brush Glaze over warm cookies.

Allow Glaze to set and dry slightly for 30 minutes before serving. Makes about 7 dozen 2" cookies.

You don't need to line up these Green Tea Ruffles by size in order to enjoy them.

Maple Crinkle Squares

What isn't to love about the combination of toasted walnuts and pure maple syrup?

½ cup unsalted butter, room temperature
½ cup shortening
1 cup granulated sugar
1 tsp. baking powder
¼ tsp. salt
1 large egg
1 tsp. pure vanilla extract
2¼ cups unbleached, all-purpose flour
½ cup finely chopped walnuts, toasted
3 tbsp. pure maple syrup
4 tbsp. maple sugar or Demerara sugar

BEV'S BITES

Maple sugar is what remains after the sap of the sugar maple is boiled for longer than is needed to create maple syrup. Once almost all the water has been boiled off, all that is left is a solid sugar. Demerara sugar is a crunchy, golden, coarse brown sugar.

Remember to buy pure maple syrup from your local producers.

Using an electric mixer, beat together the butter and shortening on medium speed to combine. Add the sugar, baking powder, and salt, beating until combined. Scrape sides of bowl.

Beat in egg and vanilla to mix. Beat in the flour to blend, then mix in the walnuts and maple syrup. Cover and chill dough for 2 hours.

Heat oven to 350 degrees.

On a lightly floured surface, roll half of the dough until ¼" thick. Using a 2½" square crinkle cookie cutter, cut dough.

Place cutouts 1" apart on ungreased cookie sheets. Sprinkle lightly with maple sugar or Demerara sugar.

Bake for 8 to 9 minutes or until edges are firm and bottoms are a light golden brown.

Cool 1 minute, then remove from cookie sheets to wire racks to cool completely. Makes about 4 dozen.

Maple Butter Cookies

The subtle sweet maple flavor in these cookies always elicits rave reviews!

1 cup unsalted butter, room temperature
1 cup granulated sugar
1/2 cup pure maple syrup
1 large egg
1 tsp. salt
3 cups unbleached, all-purpose flour

BEV'S BITES

There's a fine line between unbaked and overbaked with these delicate cookies . . . watch them carefully.

Using an electric mixer, in a large bowl, cream together the butter and sugar until light and fluffy. Scrape sides and bottom of bowl.

Beat in maple syrup and egg until mixture is well combined. Mix in salt and flour just until combined, scraping sides and bottom of bowl.

Divide dough in half and shape into 2 disks. Wrap in plastic wrap; flatten to 1/2". Chill dough for 2 hours (up to 24 hours).

Heat oven to 350 degrees. Roll dough out on a lightly floured surface to 1/8" thick, one disk at a time (keeping remaining dough refrigerated). Cut with your favorite leaf-shaped cookie cutters (maple preferred!).

Bake for 10 to 12 minutes or until edges are just beginning to turn a light golden brown.

Cool 1 minute, then remove from cookie sheets to wire racks to cool completely. Makes about 2 dozen.

Glazed Butter Cookies

These tasty cookies are easily decorated and enjoyed for any occasion.

1 cup unsalted butter, room temperature
1 cup granulated sugar
1 large egg
2 tbsp. orange juice
1 tbsp. pure vanilla extract
2½ cups unbleached, all-purpose flour
1 tsp. baking powder

GLAZE

2½ cups confectioners' sugar, sifted
2 tbsp. water
1 tbsp. unsalted butter, melted and
    cooled
1 tbsp. light corn syrup
Food color, if desired
Sprinkles or decorating sugar, if desired

Using an electric mixer, beat together the butter, sugar, and egg until creamy. Add orange juice and vanilla. Continue beating, stopping to scrape the bowl often, until well mixed. Reduce speed to low.

Add the flour and baking powder and beat until well mixed.

Divide dough in half and shape into 2 disks. Wrap in plastic wrap; flatten to ½". Chill dough for 2 hours.

Heat oven to 400 degrees. Roll dough out on a lightly floured surface to ⅛" thick, one disk at a time (keeping remaining dough refrigerated). Cut with your favorite cookie cutters.

Place 1" apart on ungreased cookie sheets. Bake for 7 to 10 minutes or until edges are a light golden brown.

Cool 1 minute, then remove from cookie sheets to wire racks to cool completely.

For the Glaze: Using an electric mixer, combine the confectioners' sugar, 2 tbsp. of water, melted butter, and corn syrup. Mix until sugar is well moistened. Beat at medium speed until smooth, adding additional water as necessary to reach desired glaze consistency. Add food color, if desired.

Glaze cooled cookies on racks set over waxed paper (to make clean up easier!). Add sprinkles or decorating sugar, if desired. Let stand until glaze hardens (4 hours up to overnight). Makes about 2½ to 3 dozen.

Butter Pecan Cookies

This delicious (and easy) butter cookie is loaded and topped with chopped pecans.

1 cup granulated sugar
1 cup unsalted butter, room temperature
2 large eggs
2 tsp. pure vanilla extract
2¾ cups unbleached, all-purpose flour
1¼ cups finely chopped pecans, toasted, divided
¼ tsp. salt
1 large egg white
1 tbsp. water

BEV'S BITES

A scalloped, round cookie cutter makes for an even more attractive cookie.

Using an electric mixer, combine sugar and butter in a large bowl and beat at medium speed until creamy, scraping bowl often.

Add eggs and vanilla and continue beating, scraping bowl often, until well mixed. Reduce speed to low and add flour, 1 cup of the pecans, and salt. Beat until blended.

Divide dough in half. Wrap and chill dough for 2 hours.

Heat oven to 350 degrees.

Roll dough out on a lightly floured surface to ¼" thickness, half at a time (keeping remaining dough refrigerated). Cut with a 2 to 2½" round cookie cutter, then cut each round in half. Place 1" apart on parchment-paper-lined cookie sheets.

Whisk together the egg white and 1 tbsp. of water in a small bowl. Brush the tops of the cookie dough lightly with the egg mixture, then sprinkle with remaining chopped pecans.

Bake for 10 to 12 minutes or until edges are a light golden brown. Makes about 5 dozen.

Crispy Chocolate Cutout Cookies

A delicate chocolate cookie (perfect for your favorite cutouts), with a sublimely crisp, light texture.

6 oz. semisweet chocolate, coarsely chopped
1 cup unsalted butter, room temperature
1½ cups granulated sugar
1 large egg
1 tsp. pure vanilla extract
2½ cups unbleached, all-purpose flour
¼ tsp. salt
½ tsp. baking soda

BEV'S BITES
Dough may be rolled on a combination of 1 part sifted cocoa powder and 2 parts sifted flour for a more chocolaty flavor.

Place the chocolate in a double boiler and melt over simmering water until melted and smooth, stirring occasionally.

Using an electric mixer, in a large bowl, combine the butter and sugar and beat on medium speed until light and fluffy. Add the egg and vanilla and beat until combined.

With the mixer on low, add the melted chocolate and stir until blended, stopping to scrape the bowl.

Mix in the flour, salt, and baking soda. Scrape down sides and bottom of bowl. Beat until the dough just comes together. Don't overmix.

Turn the dough out onto a lightly floured surface. Divide dough in half and shape into 2 disks. Wrap in plastic wrap; flatten to ½". Chill for 45 minutes to 1 hour.

Heat oven to 350 degrees. Roll dough out on a lightly floured surface to ¼ to ⅛" thick, one disk at a time (keeping remaining dough refrigerated). Cut with your favorite cookie cutters and place shapes on parchment-paper-lined cookie sheets, 1" apart.

Bake 8 to 10 minutes or until the cookies are slightly firm to the touch. Cool 1 minute, then remove from cookie sheets to wire racks to cool completely. Decorate if desired, or sprinkle with sifted confectioners' sugar and enjoy. Makes about 1 dozen large cookies.

Crispy Vanilla Cutout Cookies

A delicious, buttery cutout cookie that is a delight to decorate!

¾ cup unsalted butter
½ cup granulated sugar
1 large egg
1 tsp. pure vanilla extract
4½ cups unbleached, all-purpose flour
1 tsp. salt
1 tsp. baking powder

Using an electric mixer, in a large bowl, beat together the butter and sugar until light and fluffy.

Add the egg and vanilla, beating until combined.

Mix in the flour, salt, and baking powder. Scrape down sides and bottom of bowl. Beat until the dough just comes together. Don't overmix.

Turn the dough out onto a lightly floured surface. Divide dough in half and shape into 2 disks. Wrap in plastic wrap; flatten to ½". Chill for 45 minutes to 1 hour.

Heat oven to 350 degrees. Roll dough out on a lightly floured surface to ¼ to ⅛" thick, one disk at a time (keeping remaining dough refrigerated). Cut with your favorite cookie cutters and place shapes on parchment-paper-lined cookie sheets, 1" apart.

Bake 8 to 10 minutes or until the cookies are slightly firm to the touch. Cool 1 minute, then remove from cookie sheets to wire racks to cool completely. Decorate if desired, or sprinkle with sifted confectioners' sugar and enjoy. Makes about 2½ dozen.

Hearty Gingerbread Cookies

This cookie gets its nutty flavor from the addition of whole-wheat flour, and the added bonus of being a very easy dough to work with.

1½ cups granulated sugar
1 cup unsalted butter, room temperature
⅓ cup molasses
1 large egg
2¼ cups unbleached, all-purpose flour
1 cup whole-wheat flour
2 tsp. baking soda
½ tsp. salt
2 tsp. ground ginger
2 tsp. ground cinnamon

FROSTING AND DECORATIONS

2 cups confectioners' sugar, sifted
⅓ cup unsalted butter, room temperature
½ tsp. pure vanilla extract
1 to 2 tbsp. milk

For the Cookies: Using an electric mixer, in a large bowl, beat the sugar and butter until light and fluffy. Add the molasses and egg; blend well.

Stir in the flours, baking soda, salt, ginger, and cinnamon; mix well.

Divide dough in quarters and shape into 4 disks. Wrap in plastic wrap; flatten to ½" thick. Chill dough for 1 hour for easier handling.

Heat oven to 350 degrees. Roll dough out on a lightly floured surface to ⅛" thick, one disk at a time (keeping remaining dough refrigerated). Cut with floured gingerbread cookie cutters (house, boys, or girls).

Place cutouts 1" apart on ungreased cookie sheets. Bake for 8 to 9 minutes or until set. Cool 1 minute, then remove from cookie sheets to wire racks to cool completely.

For the Frosting: In a medium bowl, combine confectioners' sugar, butter, vanilla, and enough of the milk for desired spreading consistency, blending until smooth. Frost and decorate as desired. Allow Frosting to set. Makes about 2½ dozen.

If only suburban living were this blissful (and tasty!).

Sweet and Spicy Gingerbread Cookies

A sweet and sassy gingerbread dough, the enticing baking aromas will fill your home with a festive spirit.

¾ cup unsalted butter, room temperature
¾ cup firmly packed light brown sugar
2 tsp. ground ginger
1 tsp. finely ground black pepper
½ tsp. baking soda
¼ tsp. salt
¾ tsp. ground cinnamon
¼ tsp. ground nutmeg
1 large egg
⅓ cup molasses
2¾ cups unbleached, all-purpose flour

ROYAL ICING

2 cups confectioners' sugar, sifted
4 tsp. meringue powder
3 tbsp. cold water

Using an electric mixer, in a large bowl, beat together the butter and brown sugar until combined. Scrape down sides of the bowl, then add the ginger, pepper, baking soda, salt, cinnamon, and nutmeg; beat until combined.

Beat in the egg and molasses until combined. Add the flour, scraping sides of bowl occasionally, until mixed.

Divide dough in half and shape into 2 disks. Wrap in plastic wrap; flatten to ½". Chill dough for 4 hours (up to 24 hours) until easy to handle.

Line cookie sheets with parchment paper. Heat oven to 350 degrees.

Roll dough out on a lightly floured surface to ¼" thick, one disk at a time (keeping remaining dough refrigerated). Cut with floured gingerbread cookie cutters (house, boys, or girls).

Bake for 6 to 10 minutes (depending on shape and size) until tops of cookies appear dry. Cool 1 minute, then remove from cookie sheets to wire racks to cool completely.

For the Icing: Using an electric mixer, in a medium mixing bowl, combine the confectioners' sugar and meringue powder. Add 3 tbsp. of cold water.

Beat on low speed until mixture is combined, then beat on medium-high speed for 5 to 8 minutes or until mixture forms stiff peaks. If mixture seems too stiff while beating, add additional water cautiously, ½ tsp. at a time. Icing should be fairly thick for piping. For a thinner glaze consistency, stir in a little more water before beating. When not using, keep tightly covered with a damp towel to prevent it from drying out. Makes 2 cups.

When cookies are cool, decorate as desired. Makes about 1½ dozen.

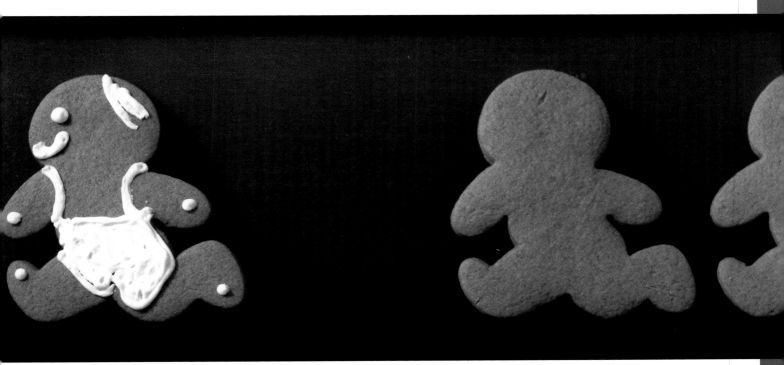

He may think he's ahead, but these Sweet and Spicy Gingerbread Cookies are catching up.

Cream-Cheese-Spiced Cutouts

Cream cheese yields cookies that are flavorful, tender, and flaky.

2$\frac{1}{4}$ **cups unbleached, all-purpose flour**
$\frac{3}{4}$ **tsp. ground cinnamon**
$\frac{1}{4}$ **tsp. ground allspice**
$\frac{1}{8}$ **tsp. freshly ground nutmeg**
$\frac{1}{8}$ **tsp. salt**
$\frac{2}{3}$ **cup unsalted butter, room temperature**
3 oz. cream cheese, room temperature
$\frac{1}{2}$ **cup granulated sugar**
3 tbsp. milk
1$\frac{1}{2}$ **tsp. fresh lemon zest, finely grated**

For Icing, Frosting, or Glaze, turn to the **Sweet Secrets** section of Cookie Basics.

In a medium bowl, stir together the flour, cinnamon, allspice, nutmeg, and salt until well combined.

Using an electric mixer, in a large bowl, beat together the butter, cream cheese, and sugar until well combined. Scrape down sides and bottom of bowl.

Beat in milk and lemon zest. Add the flour mixture, beating just until combined, stopping to scrape down the bowl.

Divide dough in half and shape into 2 disks. Wrap in plastic wrap; flatten to $\frac{1}{2}$". Chill dough for 2 to 3 hours or until firm.

Heat oven to 350 degrees. Roll dough out on a lightly floured surface to $\frac{1}{8}$" thick, one disk at a time (keeping remaining dough refrigerated). Cut with your favorite cookie cutters, preferably 2 to 2$\frac{1}{2}$" in size.

Place on ungreased cookie sheets and bake for 8 to 10 minutes or until bottoms are a light golden brown. Cool 1 minute, then remove from cookie sheets to wire racks to cool completely.

Spread desired Icing, Frosting, or Glaze over cooled cookies. Makes about 4 dozen.

Cute As a Button

Although old fashioned, thumbprint cookies can easily become an elegant addition to a cookie tray.

1 cup unsalted butter, room temperature
$^1\!/_2$ cup granulated sugar
$1^1\!/_2$ tsp. pure vanilla extract
2 cups unbleached, all-purpose flour
$^1\!/_4$ tsp. salt
$^1\!/_2$ cup apricot or raspberry fruit spread
   or seedless raspberry preserves

Using an electric mixer, in a large bowl, beat the butter and sugar until light and fluffy. Scrape sides and bottom of bowl.

Beat in vanilla, then mix in flour and salt until combined.

Wrap dough in plastic wrap; flatten to $^1\!/_2$". Chill dough for 1 hour.

Heat oven to 350 degrees. Roll dough out on a lightly floured surface to $^1\!/_2$" thick. With a $1^1\!/_2$" round cookie cutter, cut circles of dough and place 2" apart on ungreased cookie sheets.

Using your clean thumb or the back of a spoon, press a shallow well into the center of each cut out. Fill each well with about 1 tsp. of fruit spread or preserves.

Bake the cookies until the edges are a light golden brown, about 12 to 15 minutes. Cool 1 minute, then remove from cookie sheets to wire racks to cool completely. Makes about 2 dozen.

Apparently size matters to this Peanut Butter Overachiever.

Peanut Butter Overachievers

Each of these cookies could serve two. They're fun to make and even those that are not peanut butter fans enjoy their subtle tastes.

½ cup creamy peanut butter
¼ cup unsalted butter, room temperature
¼ cup shortening
1 cup firmly packed light brown sugar
1 large egg
1 tsp. pure vanilla extract
1 tsp. baking powder
1¼ cups unbleached, all-purpose flour

FILLING

¼ cup unsalted butter, room temperature
⅓ cup creamy peanut butter
3 cups confectioners' sugar, sifted
1 tsp. pure vanilla extract
1 tbsp. milk, whole or 2 percent plus
   additional as needed

BEV'S BITES

These take a little time but are fun to make, a perfect baking project with kids of all ages!

Are you artistically challenged? To make a peanut-shaped pattern, the shape should be 3" long by 1¼" wide, with an indentation of ¼" on each side in the center. You're on your way to becoming an artist.

Using an electric mixer, in a large bowl, beat together the peanut butter, butter, shortening, and brown sugar until light and fluffy. Scrape down sides and bottom of bowl.

Add the egg and vanilla, stirring to blend. Mix in the baking powder and flour. Scrape down sides and bottom of bowl.

Divide dough in half and shape into 2 disks. Wrap in plastic wrap; flatten to ½". Chill dough for 2 hours up to overnight.

While dough is chilling, it's arts and crafts time. Make a peanut-shaped pattern on heavy-duty paper and cut out.

Heat oven to 350 degrees. Roll dough out on a lightly floured surface to ⅛" thick, one disk at a time (keeping remaining dough refrigerated). Use the peanut pattern on dough and cut out with a sharp knife, placing cutouts 1½" apart on ungreased cookie sheets.

Bake for 7 to 9 minutes or just until bottoms are lightly browned. Cool 1 minute, then remove from cookie sheets to wire racks to cool completely.

For the Filling: Using an electric mixer, in a medium bowl, beat together the butter and peanut butter until well combined. Mix in the confectioners' sugar, vanilla, and milk, beating until well blended. Add additional milk if needed to reach desired spreading consistency.

Spread a generous amount of Filling carefully over the flat side of half of the cutouts. Top with remaining half of cutouts, flat side in. Gently press together and allow to set. Makes about 2 dozen.

"Limon" Cutouts

A hint of lime and a hint of lemon, all dressed up with a crisp yellow and green glaze.

½ cup unsalted butter, room temperature
3 oz. cream cheese, room temperature
1½ cups confectioners' sugar, sifted
½ tsp. baking powder
1 large egg
1 tbsp. fresh lime juice
½ tsp. fresh lemon juice
1¾ cups unbleached, all-purpose flour
1 tsp. fresh lime zest, finely grated
1 tsp. fresh lemon zest, finely grated

ICING

2 cups confectioners' sugar, sifted
1 tbsp. milk
1 tsp. fresh lime juice plus additional as
 needed
Green food coloring as needed
Yellow food coloring as needed
Yellow sprinkles and green sprinkles, if
 desired

Heat oven to 375 degrees.

Using an electric mixer, in a large bowl, beat together the butter and cream cheese to combine. Add the confectioners' sugar and baking powder; beat until combined. Scrape down sides and bottom of bowl.

Beat in the egg, lime, and lemon juice. Beat in the flour and zests. Scrape down sides and bottom of bowl.

Roll each portion of dough on a lightly floured surface until ⅛" thick. Cut with a large oval or 2" round cookie cutter. Place cutouts 1" apart on ungreased cookie sheets.

Bake for 6 to 9 minutes or until edges just begin to turn a light golden brown and appear set. Cool 1 minute, then remove from cookie sheets to wire racks to cool completely.

For the Icing: In a medium bowl, whisk together the confectioners' sugar and milk. Add lime as needed to reach desired consistency. Divide Icing in half and color half light green, the other light yellow with food coloring. Glaze cookies. If desired, sprinkle yellow sprinkles on half the glazed cookies, green sprinkles on the other half. Makes about 3 dozen.

Iced Sugar Cookies

A classic sugar cookie . . . you'll want to roll these thin for best flavor and crispness.

1 cup granulated sugar
10 tbsp. unsalted butter, room
 temperature
1½ tsp. pure vanilla extract
2 large egg whites
2½ cups unbleached, all-purpose flour
½ tsp. baking powder
¼ tsp. salt

ICING

2 cups confectioners' sugar, sifted
¼ cup milk, skim or 2 percent
½ tsp. pure vanilla extract

BEV'S BITES

Add a little color to your icing—divide the icing into portions and use a little food coloring to tint in different hues.

Using an electric mixer, in a large bowl, beat together the sugar and butter until mixture is light and fluffy. Scrape sides and bottom of bowl.

Beat in vanilla and egg whites. Gradually add in flour, baking powder, and salt, beating at low speed just until mixture is combined. Do not overbeat.

Divide dough in half and shape into 2 disks. Wrap in plastic wrap; flatten to ½". Chill dough for 1 hour.

Heat oven to 375 degrees. Roll dough out on a lightly floured surface to ¼" thick, one disk at a time (keeping remaining dough refrigerated). Cut with your favorite medium to large cookie cutters.

Place cookies 2" apart on parchment-paper-lined cookie sheets. Bake for 8 to 10 minutes or until light golden brown.

Cool 5 minutes, then remove from cookie sheets to wire racks to cool completely.

For the Icing: In a small bowl, combine the confectioners' sugar, milk, and vanilla, whisking until smooth. Spread about 1 tsp. of Icing evenly over each cookie. Let stand on wire rack until set. Makes about 2½ to 3 dozen.

Sprinkled-with-Coarse-Sugar Cookies

Coarse sugar sprinkled atop these cutouts makes for a glistening, heavenly look and taste.

¾ cup unsalted butter, room temperature
1 cup granulated sugar
2 large eggs
1 tsp. pure vanilla extract
2½ cups unbleached, all-purpose flour
1 tsp. baking powder
1 tsp. salt
1 cup (or more) coarse sugar crystals
  for sprinkling

Using an electric mixer, in a large bowl, beat together the butter and sugar until light and fluffy. Scrape bottom and sides of bowl.

Beat in the eggs and vanilla until blended.

Add the flour, baking powder, and salt, beating just until blended.

Divide dough in half and shape into 2 disks. Wrap in plastic wrap; flatten to ½". Chill dough for 2 hours (up to 24 hours).

Heat oven to 375 degrees. Roll dough out on a lightly floured surface to ⅛" thick, one disk at a time (keeping remaining dough refrigerated). Cut with your favorite cookie cutters (crescent moons, stars, and shooting stars are all favorites of mine), and place on ungreased cookie sheets.

Sprinkle the cutouts with coarse sugar and bake for 7 to 10 minutes or just until they begin to turn light golden in color. Makes about 3½ dozen.

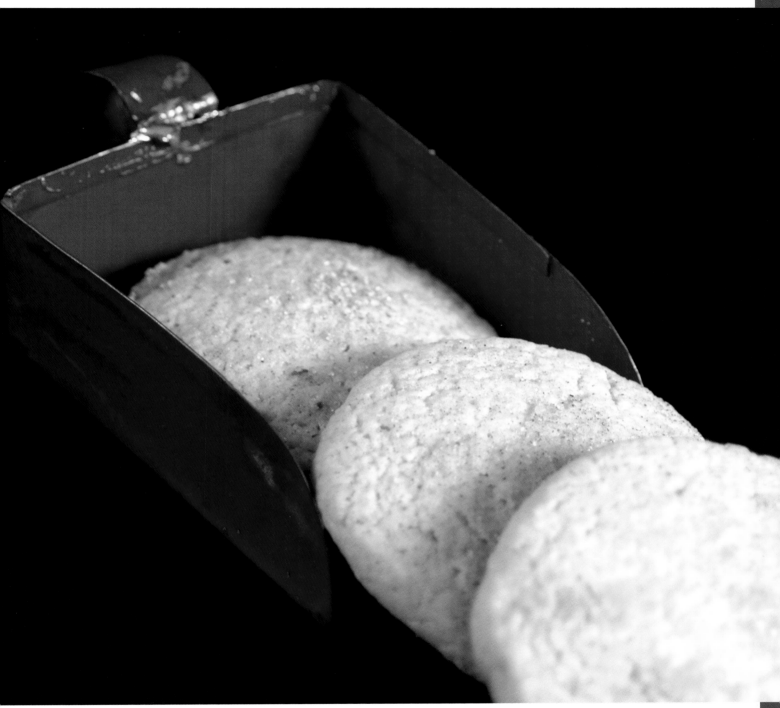

Nestled inside this antique red tin scoop (that John made as a kid for his mom) are a few Sprinkled-with-Coarse-Sugar Cookies. Oops! Did I say antique?!

Sugar Cookie Cutouts

An easy-to-work-with sugar cookie, perfect for large-quantity cutouts and a cookie decorating party!

$^1/_3$ **cup unsalted butter, room temperature**
$^1/_3$ **cup shortening**
$^3/_4$ **cup granulated sugar**
1 tsp. baking powder
Dash of salt
1 large egg
1 tsp. pure vanilla extract
2 cups unbleached, all-purpose flour

Using an electric mixer, in a large bowl, beat the butter and shortening together until combined. Scrape bottom and sides of bowl.

Add the granulated sugar, baking powder, and salt, beating until mixture is light and well blended. Scrape bottom and sides of bowl.

Beat in the egg and vanilla, then add the flour and mix just until blended. Do not overbeat.

Divide dough in half and shape into 2 disks. Wrap in plastic wrap; flatten to $^1/_2$". Chill dough for 1 to 2 hours, or until easy to handle.

Heat oven to 375 degrees. Roll dough out on a lightly floured surface to $^1/_4$" thick, one disk at a time (keeping remaining dough refrigerated). Cut with your favorite $2^1/_2$ to 3" cookie cutters.

Place on ungreased cookie sheets and bake for 8 to 10 minutes or until edges are firm and bottoms are very light golden brown.

Cool 1 minute, then remove from cookie sheets to wire racks to cool completely.

Decorate cookies, if desired, with Icing, Frosting, or Glaze from the **Sweet Secrets** section in Cookie Basics. Makes about $3^1/_2$ to 4 dozen.

A plate with ESP? How did this plate know what I was thinking about these Sugar Cookie Cutouts?!

Sour Cream Sugar Cookies with Royal Icing

Painted cutout cookies, flavored with sour cream for tender dough, make for an all-out dazzler.

½ cup unsalted butter, room temperature
1 cup granulated sugar
1 tsp. baking powder
¼ tsp. baking soda
Dash salt
½ cup sour cream
1 large egg
1 tsp. pure vanilla extract
1 tsp. fresh lemon zest, finely grated
2½ cups unbleached, all-purpose flour

ROYAL ICING

3¼ cups confectioners' sugar, sifted
3 tbsp. meringue powder
½ tsp. cream of tartar
½ cup warm water
1 tsp. pure vanilla extract

Using an electric mixer, in a large bowl, beat together the butter and sugar until light and fluffy. Add the baking powder, baking soda, and salt. Beat until combined. Scrape sides and bottom of bowl.

Beat in sour cream, egg, vanilla, and zest until combined. Add the flour, mixing just until combined. Scrape sides and bottom of bowl. Do not overbeat.

Divide dough in half and shape into 2 disks. Wrap in plastic wrap; flatten to ½". Chill dough for 1 to 2 hours or until easy to handle.

Heat oven to 375 degrees. Roll dough out on a lightly floured surface to ⅛" thick, one disk at a time (keeping remaining dough refrigerated). Cut with your favorite cookie cutters.

Place on ungreased cookie sheets. Bake for 7 to 8 minutes or just until edges are firm and cookies begin to turn a light golden color. Cool 1 minute, then remove from cookie sheets to wire racks to cool completely. Makes about 3½ to 4 dozen.

For the Icing: Whisk together the confectioners' sugar, meringue powder, and cream of tartar in a large bowl. Using an electric mixer, add the water and vanilla and beat on low speed until combined. Beat on high speed for 7 to 10 minutes or until mixture is very stiff. Cover bowl with a damp towel and plastic wrap to prevent mixture from drying out. If making ahead, refrigerate (tightly covered) for up to 2 days.

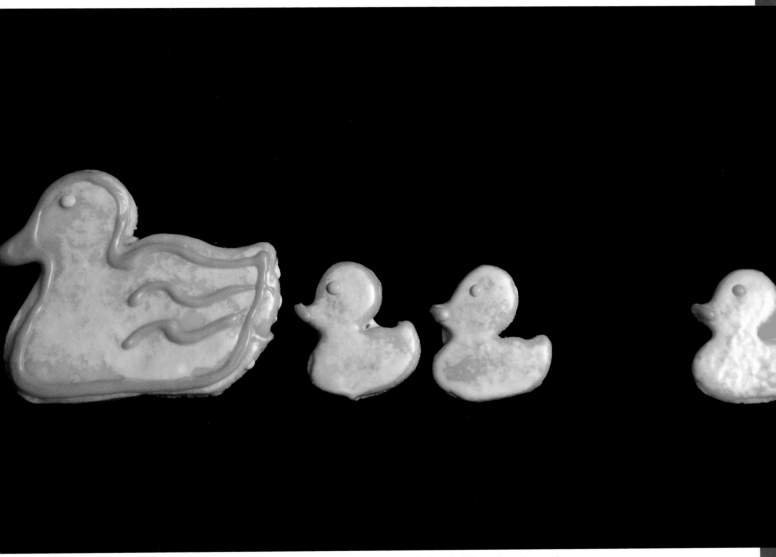

It's best to get all your ducks in a row before baking these Sour Cream Sugar Cookies with Royal Icing.

They'll Just Melt-In-Your-Mouth Sugar Cookies

Tender and moist sugar cookies, and you don't even need to pull out the cookie cutters!

½ cup unsalted butter, room temperature
½ cup shortening
2 cups granulated sugar
1 tsp. baking soda
1 tsp. cream of tartar
⅛ tsp. salt
3 large egg yolks
½ tsp. pure vanilla extract
1¾ cups unbleached, all-purpose flour

BEV'S BITES
To avoid tough and overbaked cookies, don't let the edges of the cookies brown.

Heat oven to 325 degrees. Line cookie sheets with parchment paper.

Using an electric mixer, in a large bowl, beat butter and shortening on medium-high speed until combined. Scrape sides and bottom of bowl.

Add the sugar, baking soda, cream of tartar, and salt. Beat until combined, scraping sides of bowl occasionally.

Beat in egg yolks and vanilla, then mix in flour just until well blended. Do not overbeat.

Shape dough into 1" balls. Place 2" apart on prepared cookie sheets. Bake for 9 to 12 minutes or until edges just begin to turn a light golden color and cookies appear set.

Cool 1 minute, then remove from cookie sheets to wire racks to cool completely. Makes about 3½ dozen.

Pecan Chocolate-Studded Goodies

Scooped, dropped, and devoured . . . these are the steps to these goodies!

½ cup unsalted butter, room temperature
½ cup shortening
2 cups firmly packed light brown sugar
½ cup firmly packed dark brown sugar
½ tsp. baking soda
¼ tsp. salt
2 large eggs
2½ cups unbleached, all-purpose flour
1 cup coarsely chopped pecans, toasted
½ cup semisweet chocolate, coarsely chopped into chunks
Granulated sugar for pressing cookies

Heat oven to 350 degrees. Line cookie sheets with parchment paper.

Using an electric mixer, in a large bowl, beat together the butter and shortening until combined. Scrape sides and bottom of bowl.

Add brown sugars, baking soda, and salt; beat until combined. Beat in eggs until mixed.

Mix in flour, beating just until combined. Do not overbeat. Stir in pecans and chocolate chunks.

Shape dough into balls (I used a 1" diameter cookie scoop). Place 1" apart on prepared cookie sheets. Press dough with bottom of a glass dipped in additional sugar until ½" thick.

Bake for 17 to 19 minutes or until tops are golden in color, being careful not to overbake or cookies will be dry.

Cool 2 minutes, then remove from cookie sheets to wire racks to cool completely. Makes about 4½ dozen.

Baby White Chocolate Strips

Crisp, light, sweet, a dainty-looking cookie perfect for something special!

1 cup unsalted butter, room temperature
1 large egg
3/4 cup confectioners' sugar, sifted
2 1/4 cups unbleached, all-purpose flour
Pinch of salt
1 to 2 tbsp. milk
2 tsp. pure vanilla extract

FILLING AND GLAZE

12 oz. white chocolate, coarsely
    chopped
2/3 cup assorted sprinkles

BEV'S BITES

This makes a very thick dough. If dough is too thick to press through cookie press, add additional tbsp. of milk, blending well.

Heat oven to 375 degrees.

Using an electric mixer, in a medium bowl, beat butter until light and creamy. Beat in egg until blended.

Add in sugar, flour, salt, 1 tbsp. of the milk, and vanilla; beat on low speed until well mixed. Scrape sides and bottom of bowl.

Put dough into cookie press fitted with 1" sawtooth ribbon disk. Press into 6" strips on ungreased cookie sheets. With floured knife or pizza cutter, score strips every 1".

Bake for 6 minutes or just until beginning to turn a golden brown around edges. Cut cookies along score lines.

Cool 1 minute, then remove from cookie sheets to wire racks to cool completely.

For the Filling and Glaze: While cookies are cooling, melt white chocolate in a small bowl over simmering water; stir until melted and smooth. Spread 1/2 tsp. of the melted chocolate on underside of half of the cooled cookies; top with another cookie—flat sides together.

Repeat with remaining cookies. Refrigerate 5 minutes or until set.

Place sprinkles in a dish. Dip 1/2" of end of each cookie "sandwich" in remaining white chocolate, allowing excess chocolate to drip back into bowl. Dip end into sprinkles. Place dipped-and-sprinkled cookie carefully onto waxed-paper-lined baking sheets; refrigerate to set. Makes about 4 1/2 dozen.

Aren't these Baby White Chocolate Strips just the cutest,
tastiest-looking little things?

Deep Dark Chocolate Shortbread

These simple shortbread cookies are perfectly chocolaty and not too sweet.

1 cup confectioners' sugar, sifted
1 cup unsalted butter, room temperature
2 cups unbleached, all-purpose flour
½ cup unsweetened cocoa powder, sifted
1 tsp. pure vanilla extract

GLAZE

¾ cup confectioners' sugar, sifted
1 to 2 tbsp. water
½ tsp. pure vanilla extract

Heat oven to 350 degrees.

Using an electric mixer, in a large bowl, cream together the confectioners' sugar and butter until light and fluffy.

Blend the flour, cocoa, and vanilla into creamed mixture, scraping bowl once or twice.

Divide dough into 4 parts. Roll each part on waxed paper into 10x1½" strips (using a light sprinkle of cocoa powder to dust rolling pin if needed). Gently lift strips with floured hands and transfer to ungreased cookie sheets.

Bake for 13 to 14 minutes or until not soft to the touch. Cool for 2 minutes, then cut into 1" strips.

Transfer strips to a wire rack to cool completely. Set wire rack over waxed paper and make Glaze.

For the Glaze: In a small bowl, whisk together the sugar, water, and vanilla extract until Glaze is a drizzle consistency.

Drizzle in a decorative fashion across cookies. Allow to set. Makes about 3½ dozen.

Stack 'em high and eat 'em quickly before these Deep Dark Chocolate Shortbreads are gone!

Chocolate Minties

I love to eat these the way I've always enjoyed my favorite Girl Scout cookies—right out of the freezer! Crush them and stir them into slightly softened vanilla ice cream for a dazzling, mint-inspired dessert.

1 cup unbleached, all-purpose flour
½ cup unsweetened cocoa powder, sifted
¼ tsp. baking powder
⅛ tsp. salt
6 tbsp. unsalted butter, room temperature
½ cup granulated sugar
1 large egg
½ tsp. pure vanilla extract
8 oz. bittersweet chocolate, coarsely chopped
¼ tsp. plus ⅛ tsp. pure peppermint extract

BEV'S BITES

No double boiler? A bowl that fits over the top of a saucepan will work; just be sure it fits snugly so steam doesn't creep up the sides and into your chocolate mixture, which will seize and ruin the chocolate!

Heat oven to 350 degrees.

Combine in a medium bowl the flour, cocoa powder, baking powder, and salt; set aside.

Using an electric mixer, beat the butter and sugar until light and fluffy. Add the egg and vanilla, beating to combine.

Add the flour mixture, mixing on low just until combined, stopping once or twice to scrape down the sides of the bowl.

Shape dough into ½" balls and place, 2" apart, on ungreased baking sheets. Flatten with bottom of a glass to ¼" thick. Bake for 8 to 10 minutes until just firm to the touch.

Cool 1 minute, then remove from cookie sheets to wire racks to cool completely.

For the mintie part, combine chocolate and peppermint extract in a double boiler set over simmering water. Stir until melted and combined. Remove from heat and wipe sides of double boiler top to remove any water.

Line baking sheets with waxed paper. Quickly dip the cookies into the chocolate mixture, coating as much of the top of the cookie as possible, tapping to remove any excess chocolate before placing on waxed paper. When all cookies are dipped, chill to set chocolate coating. Makes about 3 dozen.

Simply Pressed Sugar Cookies

If rolling out sugar cookie dough is not your thing, then these simple pressed cookies are perfect.

1 cup unsalted butter, room temperature
1 cup granulated sugar, divided
$\frac{1}{2}$ cup firmly packed light brown sugar
$\frac{1}{2}$ tsp. pure vanilla extract
1 large egg
2 cups unbleached, all-purpose flour
$\frac{1}{2}$ tsp. baking soda
$\frac{1}{2}$ tsp. salt

Heat oven to 350 degrees.

Using an electric mixer, beat the butter, $\frac{1}{2}$ cup of the sugar, and brown sugar until light and fluffy.

Add vanilla and egg; beat until well combined.

Stir in flour, baking soda, and salt; mix well. Shape dough into 1" balls. Place 2" apart on ungreased cookie sheets. Press dough with bottom of a glass dipped in remaining $\frac{1}{2}$ cup of sugar.

Bake for 8 to 12 minutes or until cookies are a light golden brown in color.

Cool 1 minute, then remove from cookie sheets to wire racks to cool completely. Makes about 4 dozen.

(Big As A) Sunflower Cookies

If you like large cookies that are crisp, sugary, and crunchy, it's time to heat your oven.

3 cups unbleached, all-purpose flour
1 cup firmly packed light brown sugar
1 cup firmly packed dark brown sugar
1 tsp. baking soda
1 tsp. baking powder
1 cup unsalted butter, room temperature
1 cup shortening
1 cup sunflower seeds, roasted
1 tsp. pure vanilla extract
Granulated sugar for pressing dough

BEV'S BITES

To roast sunflower seeds, place a single layer of raw shelled kernels in a shallow pan. Roast in a 300-degree oven for 30 to 40 minutes or until brown and crisp. Stir occasionally. Remove from the oven. Place the seeds on absorbent paper. Salt to taste. Store in tightly covered container.

So how does the sugar stick to the bottom of the glass? There are two tricks to try: I prefer to brush the bottom of the glass lightly with water, then quickly press into sugar to adhere. Alternately, you can spray (ever so lightly) the bottom of the glass with a vegetable cooking spray, then quickly press into sugar to adhere. Do either of these only as necessary.

Heat oven to 350 degrees.

Combine the flour, brown sugars, baking soda, and baking powder in a large mixing bowl, whisking together to blend well.

Using an electric mixer (a pastry cutter or two forks), cut the butter and shortening into the flour mixture to form a soft dough.

Stir in sunflower seeds and vanilla; mix well.

Shape dough into large balls (I used a 2" diameter cookie scoop). Place 5" apart on ungreased cookie sheets. Press dough with bottom of a flat glass dipped in additional sugar.

Bake for 10 to 12 minutes, or until light golden brown in color.

Cool 5 minutes, then remove from cookie sheets to wire racks to cool completely. Makes about 1½ dozen.

No weeding required! Enjoy these (Big As A) Sunflower Cookies,
fresh from your kitchen, today.

Almond Toffee Crunch Cookies

Toasted almond pieces and the crunch of toffee in a shortbreadlike cookie, oh my!

1 cup granulated sugar
1 cup confectioners' sugar, sifted
1 cup unsalted butter, room temperature
1 cup vegetable oil (such as canola or extra light olive oil)
1 tsp. almond extract
2 large eggs
4½ cups unbleached, all-purpose flour
1 tsp. baking soda
1 tsp. salt
1 tsp. cream of tartar
1⅔ cups coarsely chopped almonds, lightly toasted
8 to 10 oz. toffee bits
Granulated sugar for rolling and pressing dough

Heat oven to 350 degrees.

Using an electric mixer, in a large bowl, blend together the sugars, butter, and oil until well combined.

Add almond extract and eggs; mix well. Blend in the flour, baking soda, salt, and cream of tartar.

Stir in the almonds and toffee bits, mixing well to distribute.

Cover and chill dough for 1 hour. Scoop dough into large tbsp. size balls; roll in sugar.

Place 5" apart on ungreased cookie sheets. Press dough with bottom of a glass dipped in additional sugar. Bake for 14 to 19 minutes or until a light golden brown around edges.

Cool 1 minute, then remove from cookie sheets to wire racks to cool completely. Makes about 6 dozen.

*Someone wasn't paying attention when they left one last
Almond Toffee Crunch Cookie alone.*

Butterscotch Candy Shortbread Cookies

Crispy and buttery with a hint of butterscotch flavor, these cookies are sure to become cookie jar favorites!

1 cup unsalted butter, room temperature
¼ cup granulated sugar
¼ cup crushed butterscotch candy
1 tsp. pure vanilla extract
2 cups unbleached, all-purpose flour
¼ cup cornstarch
Additional sugar for pressing dough

FROSTING

1 cup confectioners' sugar, sifted
1 to 2 tbsp. milk
½ tsp. pure vanilla extract
2 tbsp. crushed butterscotch candy

Heat oven to 300 degrees. Line cookie sheets with parchment paper.

Using an electric mixer, in a large mixing bowl, beat together the butter and sugar until light and fluffy. Add the crushed candy and vanilla.

Mix in the flour and cornstarch. Scrape down sides and bottom of bowl.

Shape dough into 1" size balls. Press dough with bottom of a glass dipped in additional sugar.

Bake for 25 to 30 minutes or until bottoms begin to turn a light golden brown. Cool for 5 minutes, then remove from cookie sheets to wire racks to cool completely.

For the Frosting: Combine the confectioners' sugar, milk, and vanilla in a small bowl, mixing until smooth. Drizzle atop cooled cookies, then sprinkle crushed candy on top. Makes about 3 dozen.

Orange Butter Cookies

A buttery mix of a burst of orange with a brush of chocolate!

¾ cup unsalted butter, room temperature
1 cup granulated sugar
1 tsp. pure vanilla extract
1 large egg
½ tsp. salt
2 tbsp. fresh orange zest, finely grated
1 tsp. baking powder
2 cups cake flour, sifted
2 tbsp. confectioners' sugar, sifted

GLAZE

2 tbsp. unsalted butter
1 tbsp. light corn syrup
3 oz. semisweet chocolate, coarsely
   chopped

BEV'S BITES

So how does the sugar stick to the bottom of the glass? Here's a trick to try: For this recipe, spray (ever so lightly) the bottom of the glass with a vegetable cooking spray, then quickly press into sugar to adhere. Do this only as necessary.

Heat oven to 350 degrees.

Using an electric mixer, in a large bowl, cream together the butter and sugar until light.

Add the vanilla, egg, salt, and zest; mix well. Mix in the baking powder and flour until thoroughly blended. Scrape down sides and bottom of bowl.

Cover and refrigerate the dough for several hours for easier handling.

Shape dough into 1" balls and place them 3" apart on ungreased cookie sheets. Press dough to ¼" thick with bottom of a glass dipped in the sifted confectioners' sugar.

Bake for 10 to 12 minutes or until the edges of the cookies are a light golden brown. Cool 1 minute, then remove from cookie sheets to wire racks to cool completely.

For the Glaze: In a small saucepan, combine the butter, corn syrup, and chocolate. Cook over low heat, stirring, until melted and smooth. Remove from heat.

Brush Glaze over half of each cookie. Cool on waxed paper until glaze is set. Makes about 3 dozen.

*The extra plates are just in case two of the
Orange Crescents aren't enough.*

Orange Crescents

A delicate, flavorful cookie that's well worth the effort and a great way to practice your patience!

1 cup unsalted butter, room temperature
1 large egg
1½ tbsp. fresh orange zest, finely grated
1 tbsp. fresh orange juice
¾ cup confectioners' sugar, sifted
2 cups unbleached, all-purpose flour
¼ tsp. salt

GLAZE

⅔ cup confectioners' sugar, sifted
1 tbsp. plus 1 tsp. fresh orange juice

Using an electric mixer, in a large bowl, beat the butter, egg, zest, and orange juice until smooth. Scrape down sides and bottom of bowl.

Beat in confectioners' sugar, flour, and salt until blended. Cover and chill for 2 hours.

Heat oven to 350 degrees. Form 1 rounded tsp. of dough into a 3" log, then bend into a crescent. Place on ungreased cookie sheets. Repeat with remaining dough.

Bake for 9 to 10 minutes or until edges are beginning to turn a light golden in color and tops are beginning to crack ever so slightly.

Cool 5 minutes, then remove from cookie sheets to wire racks to cool completely.

For the Glaze: In a small bowl, whisk together the confectioners' sugar and orange juice until smooth.

Place wire racks with cookies atop sheets of waxed paper (for easier clean up!). Drizzle Glaze atop cookies. Makes about 2½ dozen.

NEW CLASSICS

Yes, one bite and you'll agree—these are Much Better Than Fruitcake (Bars).

So what are new classics?

Cookies have phases, just like the moon, but there are cookies that endure—recipes that you turn to again and again to bake because you're in the mood, your family has requested them, or you've been asked to bring that special cookie you make to a bridal shower or for a cookie exchange.

Enter some new cookies, destined to become classics as well. They're tweaks and twists to old favorites (oatmeal cookies and chocolate chip cookies), they're more modern flavors we've come to know and love (chai and ginger), or they're something we know we'll make again and again—a "signature" cookie of our own (flax and maple). Above all, don't forget that cookies make us smile, too (pb&js and yin yang).

Got dough?

Lacy Cranberry Oatmeal Cookies with Orange Glaze

A delightfully crispy oatmeal cookie and a surprise glaze!

1½ cups unsalted butter, room
  temperature
1 cup firmly packed light brown sugar
1 cup granulated sugar
1 large egg
1½ tsp. pure vanilla extract
3 cups old-fashioned rolled oats (not
  quick oats)
1½ cups unbleached, all-purpose flour
2½ tsp. baking soda
¾ tsp. salt
1 cup dried cranberries, snipped into
  small pieces

GLAZE

2 cups confectioners' sugar, sifted
2 tbsp. fresh orange juice
1 tsp. fresh orange zest, finely grated

BEV'S BITES

A sharp pair of kitchen shears works well
for snipping the cranberries. Dip them in
hot water between snips to keep the cranberries from sticking.

Heat oven to 350 degrees. Line cookie sheets with parchment paper.

Using an electric mixer, in a large bowl, cream the butter and sugars together until mixture is light and fluffy. Scrape down sides and bottom of bowl.

Mix in egg and vanilla until blended. Add the oats, flour, baking soda, and salt, stirring just until mixed. Do not overbeat. Stir in the dried cranberries.

Drop dough by rounded teaspoonfuls onto prepared cookie sheets, spacing 2" apart.

Bake for 8 to 11 minutes or just until cookies are light golden brown around edges. Cool 1 minute, then remove from cookie sheets to wire racks to cool completely.

Set wire racks atop waxed paper.

For the Glaze: In a small bowl, whisk together the confectioners' sugar, orange juice, and zest until desired glazing consistency. Drizzle Glaze over cookies. Makes about 4½ dozen.

Cranberry-Orange Oatmeal Cookies

A flavorful oatmeal cookie with walnuts, dried cranberries, and a hint of fresh orange zest.

10 tbsp. unsalted butter, room temperature

½ cup granulated sugar

6 tbsp. firmly packed light brown sugar

1 tsp. fresh orange juice

½ tsp. pure vanilla extract

2 tsp. ground cinnamon

2 tbsp. fresh orange zest, finely grated (about 2 oranges)

2 large eggs

¾ cup plus 2 tbsp. unbleached, all-purpose flour

¾ tsp. baking soda

¾ tsp. salt

1¼ cups old-fashioned rolled oats (not quick oats)

¾ cup coarsely chopped walnuts, toasted

1 cup dried cranberries

Heat oven to 375 degrees. Line cookie sheets with parchment paper.

Using an electric mixer, in a large bowl, beat on medium-high speed the butter, granulated sugar and brown sugar, orange juice, vanilla, cinnamon, and zest together until light and fluffy. Scrape down sides and bottom of bowl.

Add the eggs and mix on medium speed until blended.

Mix in the flour, baking soda, and salt until combined. Scrape down sides and bottom of bowl.

Stir in the oats, walnuts, and cranberries to blend.

Scoop and drop the dough using a 2" cookie scoop (equal to about 3 tbsp.), spacing them 2" apart on the prepared sheets. (Cookies will spread.)

Bake for 12 to 14 minutes or until the edges are golden with slightly puffed centers. Cool 1 minute, then remove from cookie sheets to wire racks to cool completely. Makes about 18 large cookies.

The perfect pick-me-up—a tall glass of organic milk and two Cranberry-Orange Oatmeal Cookies. I'm feeling perkier already!

Oatmeal, Cranberry, Cherry, and Raisin Cookies

I love this combination of oats and dried fruits . . . perfect for a snack on the go.

¾ cup granulated sugar
¼ cup firmly packed light brown sugar
½ cup unsalted butter, room temperature
½ tsp. pure vanilla extract
1 large egg
¾ cup unbleached, all-purpose flour
½ tsp. baking soda
½ tsp. ground cinnamon
¼ tsp. salt
1½ cups old-fashioned rolled oats
½ cup seedless raisins
¼ cup dried cranberries
¼ cup dried cherries

Heat oven to 375 degrees. Line cookie sheets with parchment paper.

Using an electric mixer, in a large bowl, beat together the granulated and brown sugars and the butter until light and fluffy. Scrape down sides and bottom of bowl. Add the vanilla and egg, mixing until well combined.

Add the flour, baking soda, cinnamon, and salt; mix until well combined. Stir in the oats, raisins, cranberries, and cherries.

Drop dough by rounded teaspoonfuls 2" apart on prepared cookie sheets. Bake for 8 to 11 minutes or just until edges are a light golden brown.

Cool 1 minute, then remove from cookie sheets to wire racks to cool completely. Makes about 3 dozen.

Soft and Chewy Oatmeal Cookies

A touch of whole-wheat flour makes these soft, chewy oatmeal cookies extra special.

1 cup firmly packed light brown sugar
1 cup firmly packed dark brown sugar
$\frac{1}{2}$ cup shortening
$\frac{1}{2}$ cup unsalted butter, room temperature
1 tsp. pure vanilla extract
2 large eggs
1 cup unbleached, all-purpose flour
1 cup whole-wheat flour
1 tsp. baking powder
3 cups old-fashioned rolled oats (not quick oats)

Heat oven to 350 degrees.

Using an electric mixer, in a large bowl, combine the brown sugars, shortening, and butter, beating until light and fluffy.

Add the vanilla and eggs, mixing until well combined.

Mix in the unbleached, all-purpose and wheat flours and the baking powder until blended; stir in the oats.

Drop dough by heaping tablespoonfuls 2" apart on ungreased cookie sheets.

Bake for 11 to 15 minutes or just until cookies are a light golden brown. Cool 1 minute, then remove from cookie sheets to wire racks to cool completely. Makes about 2 dozen.

Ohio Maple Oatmeal Cookies

This delightful twist on an oatmeal cookie features Ohio's pure maple syrup. Find a local producer in your state and enjoy these easy to make treats today!

½ cup unsalted butter, room temperature
1½ cups unbleached, all-purpose flour, divided
1 cup Ohio pure maple syrup
1 large egg
¼ cup milk
2 tsp. baking powder
¼ tsp. salt
1½ cups old-fashioned rolled oats (not quick cooking)
½ cup seedless raisins
½ cup chopped walnuts, toasted

Heat oven to 350 degrees. Line cookie sheets with parchment paper.

Using an electric mixer, in a large bowl, beat the butter with half the flour. Scrape down sides and bottom of bowl.

Add the maple syrup, egg, milk, baking powder, and salt. Beat until well combined, stopping to scrape down sides and bottom of bowl occasionally.

Stir in remaining flour and oats. Add the raisins and walnuts, mixing until blended.

Drop dough by heaping teaspoonfuls 2" apart onto prepared cookie sheets. Bake for 12 to 14 minutes or until edges are a light golden brown.

Cool 1 minute, then remove from cookie sheets to wire racks to cool completely. Makes about 3½ dozen.

Maple Doodles

It's time to update that snicker doodle with pure maple syrup and a little maple sugar for a delightful twist.

$\frac{1}{3}$ **cup unsalted butter, room temperature**
$\frac{2}{3}$ **cup pure maple syrup**
$\frac{3}{4}$ **tsp. baking soda**
$\frac{1}{2}$ **tsp. cream of tartar**
$\frac{1}{4}$ **tsp. salt**
1 large egg
1$\frac{1}{2}$ cups unbleached, all-purpose flour

TOPPING

5 tbsp. maple sugar
1$\frac{1}{2}$ tsp. ground cinnamon

BEV'S BITES

Maple sugar, about twice as sweet as granulated sugar, is the result of continuing to boil the sap from maple trees until the liquid has almost entirely evaporated.

Heat oven to 375 degrees. Line cookie sheets with parchment paper.

Using an electric mixer, in a large bowl, beat the butter, maple syrup, baking soda, cream of tartar, and salt until well blended. Scrape down sides and bottom of bowl.

Beat in egg until combined. Add in flour, mixing until blended.

For the Topping: In a small bowl, stir together the maple sugar and cinnamon.

Drop dough by rounded teaspoonfuls 2" apart onto the prepared cookie sheets. Sprinkle tops of these dough mounds with a little of the sugar and cinnamon mixture, pressing lightly with fingers so mixture will adhere.

Bake for 9 to 11 minutes or until edges are firm to the touch.

Cool 1 minute, then remove from cookie sheets to wire racks to cool completely. Makes about 2$\frac{1}{2}$ dozen.

Live and Let Chai Cookies

The combination of black tea and lots of spices make a sensational cookie.

1 cup unsalted butter, room temperature
1 tsp. loose-leaf black tea
½ cup confectioners' sugar, sifted
2 cups unbleached, all-purpose flour
1 tsp. ground cardamom
1½ tsp. ground allspice
1 tsp. ground cinnamon
1 tsp. freshly ground nutmeg
½ tsp. ground ginger
¼ tsp. ground cloves
½ tsp. salt
4 tsp. pure vanilla extract
2 large egg yolks

COATING

1½ cups confectioners' sugar, sifted
½ tsp. ground allspice
½ tsp. ground cinnamon

Heat oven to 350 degrees. Using an electric mixer, in a large bowl, beat the butter, tea, and confectioners' sugar until blended. Scrape sides and bottom of bowl.

Mix in the flour, cardamom, allspice, cinnamon, nutmeg, ginger, cloves, salt, vanilla, and egg yolks, beating until well blended.

Shape dough by tablespoonfuls into balls. Place on ungreased cookie sheets 1" apart.

Bake 12 to 14 minutes or just until a light golden brown. Cool 5 minutes.

For the Coating: In a shallow bowl, combine the confectioners' sugar, allspice, and cinnamon, whisking until combined.

Working in batches, gently roll the warm cookies in the Coating mixture. Cool cookies on racks for 4 minutes, then reroll. Makes about 3 ½ dozen.

Scents of Cinnamon Cookies

Perfect as a light dessert, this easy to make cookie is bursting with cinnamon flavor.

$^{1}/_{2}$ **cup confectioners' sugar, sifted**
1 cup unsalted butter, room temperature
1 tsp. pure vanilla extract
2 cups unbleached, all-purpose flour
1 cup finely chopped pecans
$^{3}/_{4}$ **tsp. ground cinnamon**
$^{1}/_{8}$ **tsp. salt**

COATING

$^{1}/_{2}$ **cup confectioners' sugar, sifted**
1 tsp. ground cinnamon

Heat oven to 325 degrees.

Using an electric mixer, in a large bowl, combine the confectioners' sugar, butter, and vanilla, beating until light and fluffy.

Add the flour, nuts, cinnamon, and salt; mix well.

Shape dough into 1" balls. Place 1" apart on ungreased cookie sheets.

Bake for 14 to 16 minutes or until set but not brown. Immediately remove from cookie sheets and cool on wire racks for 2 minutes.

For the Coating: In a shallow bowl, combine the confectioners' sugar and the cinnamon, whisking to blend.

Roll warm cookies in coating. Cool 10 minutes, then reroll. Cool on a wire rack until completely cooled. Makes about 4 dozen.

No one believes these Cinnamon Sugar Whole-Wheat Crackles are made with whole-wheat flour (so don't even bother telling them)!

Cinnamon Sugar Whole-Wheat Crackles

These cookies are sensational, with the whole-wheat flour giving them a nutty, fresh flavor.

1 cup granulated sugar
½ cup unsalted butter, room temperature
2 tbsp. milk, whole or 2 percent
1 tsp. fresh lemon zest, finely grated
1 tsp. pure vanilla extract
1 large egg
1¾ cups whole-wheat flour
1 tsp. baking powder
½ tsp. baking soda
½ tsp. salt
½ tsp. ground cinnamon

COATING

4 tbsp. granulated sugar
1 tsp. ground cinnamon

Using an electric mixer, in a large bowl, beat together 1 cup of the sugar with the butter until light and fluffy. Scrape down sides and bottom of bowl.

Add milk, zest, vanilla, and egg; blend well.

Mix in the flour, baking powder, baking soda, salt, and cinnamon just until combined. Do not overbeat. Cover and chill dough for 1 hour.

Heat oven to 375 degrees.

For the Coating: In a small bowl, whisk together the sugar and the cinnamon; set aside.

Shape dough into 1" balls; roll in cinnamon-sugar mixture. Place 2" apart on ungreased cookie sheets.

Bake for 8 to 10 minutes or just until cookies are a light golden brown. Cool 1 minute, then remove from cookie sheets to wire racks to cool completely. Makes about 2½ dozen.

Chunks of Chocolate Cookies

Lots of vanilla and chunks of bittersweet chocolate make for a chocolate chip cookie with a twist and a turn.

½ cup unsalted butter, room temperature
½ cup firmly packed light brown sugar
¼ cup plus 2½ tbsp. granulated sugar
1 large egg
2 tsp. pure vanilla extract or vanilla bean paste
1⅔ cups unbleached, all-purpose flour
¾ tsp. baking soda
1 tsp. salt
8½ oz. bittersweet chocolate, coarsely chopped

BEV'S BITES

Vanilla bean paste can be substituted for the pure vanilla extract, giving it a more intense vanilla flavor. Vanilla bean paste is pure vanilla with natural vanilla bean seeds in a unique, convenient, paste form . . . like scraping the seeds from vanilla bean pods, without all the work!

Heat oven to 350 degrees. Line cookie sheets with parchment paper.

Using an electric mixer, in a large bowl, beat together the butter and the brown and granulated sugars until light and fluffy. Scrape sides and bottom of bowl.

Add the egg and vanilla, beating to blend. Stir in the flour, baking soda, and salt, mixing just until blended. Scrape sides and bottom of bowl. Stir in the chocolate pieces.

Using a 2" diameter cookie scoop (about 3 tablespoonfuls), scoop the cookie dough onto cookie sheets spacing 2" apart.

Bake for 8 to 10 minutes or just until cookies are a light golden brown. Cool 1 minute, then remove from cookie sheets to wire racks to cool completely. Makes about 1½ dozen.

A Little Bit Lighter Chocolate Chip Cookies

Using plain Greek yogurt in these cookies reduces the fat but keeps the flavor.

½ cup granulated sugar
½ cup firmly packed light brown sugar
¼ cup unsalted butter, room temperature
¼ cup shortening
½ cup plain Greek yogurt, 2 percent
   or skim
1½ tsp. pure vanilla extract
1¾ cups unbleached, all-purpose flour
½ tsp. baking soda
½ tsp. salt
1 cup semisweet chocolate, coarsely
   chopped or semisweet chocolate chips

BEV'S BITES

My favorite brand of Greek yogurt is
Fage®, and it's available in whole milk, 2
percent, or skim. I traditionally use the 2
percent. If not available in your area, a
good-quality nonfat plain yogurt will work
in this recipe.

My shortening of choice is Earth Balance®
shortening (stick). This shortening contains no trans-fatty acids, nothing artificial,
and is nonhydrogenated, with non-GMO
ingredients.

Heat oven to 375 degrees.

Using an electric mixer, in a large bowl, beat together the granulated and brown sugars, butter, and shortening until light and
fluffy.

Scrape sides and bottom of bowl. Add the yogurt and vanilla;
blend well.

Mix in the flour, baking soda, and salt until blended, then stir in
the chocolate pieces or chips.

Drop dough by rounded teaspoonfuls 2" apart onto ungreased
cookie sheets.

Bake for 10 to 15 minutes or just until cookies are a light golden
brown. Cool 1 minute, then remove from cookie sheets to wire
racks to cool completely. Makes about 5½ dozen.

No-Flour Chocolate Cookies

Who says a flourless chocolate treat just has to be a cake? This large, crisp, and very chocolaty cookie will set that myth aside.

¾ **cup unsweetened cocoa powder, sifted**
2½ **cups confectioners' sugar, sifted**
Pinch of salt
2 **cups toasted walnuts, finely chopped**
1 **tbsp. pure vanilla extract**
4 **large egg whites, room temperature**

Heat oven to 350 degrees. Line cookie sheets with parchment paper.

Using an electric mixer, in a large bowl, mix together the cocoa powder, confectioners' sugar, and salt. Add walnuts; mix to blend.

In a small bowl, whisk together the vanilla and egg whites.

With mixer on low speed, slowly add egg mixture to dry ingredients. Scrape bottom and sides of bowl. Turn speed to medium and mix for 2 minutes to blend well.

Using a ¼ cup measure or equivalent cookie scoop, drop dough onto prepared cookie sheets, spacing at least 3" apart (these cookies *s p r e a d!*).

Place cookie sheet in oven and immediately turn oven to 325 degrees. Bake for 12 to 14 minutes or until thin cracks appear on the cookies' surface.

Cool completely on a wire rack before attempting to remove cookies. Makes about 1 dozen.

Close your eyes and take a bite. There's a light crunch and intense chocolate flavor in these No-Flour Chocolate Cookies you'll love.
(It's okay to open your eyes now.)

Chocolate Chocolate Babies

An irresistible chocolate cookie, with a crunch and a snap, perfect for a crowd as one batch makes an abundant amount.

2 cups granulated sugar plus additional for rolling dough
1 cup firmly packed light brown sugar
1½ cups unsalted butter, room temperature
2 tsp. pure vanilla extract
3 large eggs
6 oz. bittersweet chocolate, melted and cooled
4 cups unbleached, all-purpose flour
2 tsp. baking soda
1 tsp. salt

BEV'S BITES

These are my Ginger Babies gone wild . . . with lots of chocolate!

Heat oven to 350 degrees. Line cookie sheets with parchment paper.

Using an electric mixer, in a large bowl, beat together the granulated and brown sugars and the butter until light and fluffy. Scrape sides and bottom of bowl.

Add vanilla, eggs, and the melted and cooled chocolate; blend well.

Add flour, baking soda, and salt; mix until combined. Cover and chill dough for 4 hours (up to overnight).

Shape dough into 1" balls (or smaller, depending on how baby-ish you want these cookies!). Roll in additional granulated sugar to coat well.

Place 2" apart on prepared cookie sheets. Bake for 8 to 12 minutes or until set. (These cookies will puff and then flatten during baking.)

Cool 1 minute, then remove from cookie sheets to wire racks to cool completely. Makes about 5½ dozen.

Chocolate Cookies with Chocolate

Chocolate melted into the batter, then chocolate chunks tossed in just for good measure.

6 oz. unsweetened chocolate
1/4 cup unsalted butter, room temperature
2 large eggs
1 1/3 cups granulated sugar
1 tsp. finely ground coffee
1 tsp. pure vanilla extract
1/3 cup unbleached, all-purpose flour
1/4 tsp. baking powder
1/4 tsp. salt
4 oz. bittersweet chocolate, chopped into small chunks
1/2 cup walnut pieces, toasted, then coarsely chopped

BEV'S BITES
Toast walnuts in a dry skillet over low heat just until fragrant, watching carefully so they don't burn.

Heat oven to 350 degrees. Line cookie sheets with parchment paper.

In a small saucepan, over low heat, melt the 6 oz. of chocolate with the butter, stirring until mixture is smooth. Remove from heat.

Using an electric mixer, in a large bowl, beat together the eggs, sugar, coffee, and vanilla until mixture is well combined. Beat on high speed for 8 minutes until mixture has thickened.

Turn the mixer to low, then slowly add the melted chocolate/butter mixture. Scrape down the sides and bottom of bowl.

Add the flour, baking powder, and salt, stirring just until blended. Do not overbeat. Add in the chocolate chunks and walnut pieces.

Drop the dough by tablespoonfuls, spacing 2" apart, on prepared cookie sheets. Bake for 11 to 13 minutes, until top looks slightly crispy and almost done. Do not overbake—thus creating a crusty outside and a soft center.

Cool 1 minute, then remove from cookie sheets to wire racks to cool completely. Makes about 2 dozen.

Don't read too much into this one. Just enjoy the cookie!

Yin Yang Chocolate Cookies

Two doughs combine to create a unity of opposites . . . be at peace with the cookies!

2 tbsp. instant coffee crystals
3 tbsp. half-and-half, divided
1 cup unsalted butter, room temperature
²/₃ cup granulated sugar
²/₃ cup firmly packed light brown sugar
1 tsp. baking soda
¼ tsp. salt
1 large egg
1 tsp. pure vanilla extract
2¼ cups unbleached, all-purpose flour
¼ cup unsweetened cocoa powder, sifted
½ cup white chocolate, finely chopped into pieces
½ cup semisweet chocolate, finely chopped into pieces

Heat oven to 375 degrees. In a small bowl, dissolve coffee crystals in 1 tbsp. of the half-and-half. Set aside.

Using an electric mixer, in a large bowl, beat together the butter, sugars, baking soda, and salt on medium-high speed until well combined. Scrape down sides and bottom of bowl.

Beat in the coffee mixture, egg, and vanilla until combined.

Add the flour, mixing until blended. Divide the dough in half; set one portion aside.

Stir in the remaining 2 tbsp. of the half-and-half and the cocoa powder into one portion of dough. Stir white chocolate pieces into this chocolate dough.

Stir the semisweet pieces into the plain dough.

Drop scant tsp. of each dough side by side onto an ungreased cookie sheet. Press dough pairs together. Bake for 10 to 12 minutes or just until set.

Cool 1 minute, then remove from cookie sheets to wire racks to cool completely. Makes about 4½ dozen.

Chocolate-Dipped Shortbread Logs with Hazelnuts

A crunchy shortbread stick and a hazelnut-and-chocolate dip make for a perfect combination.

½ cup unsalted butter, room temperature
½ cup confectioners' sugar
½ cup finely ground, skinned, and toasted hazelnuts
1 tsp. pure vanilla extract
1 cup unbleached, all-purpose flour
½ tsp. baking powder
¼ tsp. salt

DIP

2 oz. semisweet chocolate, coarsely chopped
2 oz. milk chocolate, coarsely chopped
⅓ cup coarsely chopped, skinned, and toasted hazelnuts

BEV'S BITES

To skin hazelnuts: place hazelnuts on an ungreased jellyroll pan and bake at 325 degrees for 20 to 25 minutes. Immediately dump into a clean kitchen towel, spreading into a single layer. Working quickly, fold half of the towel over hazelnuts and rub continuously back and forth over hazelnuts to remove their skins. Remove skinned hazelnuts to plate to cool.

Heat oven to 325 degrees. Line cookie sheets with parchment paper.

Using an electric mixer, in a large bowl, beat butter and sugar until light and fluffy. Scrape sides and bottom of bowl.

Beat in hazelnuts and vanilla. Add flour, baking powder, and salt, stirring just until combined. Do not overbeat.

Form 1 tbsp. of dough into 3" logs. Place on prepared cookie sheets, finishing their shaping on cookie sheet. Space 1" apart.

Bake for 22 to 26 minutes or until a light golden brown and no longer soft. Cool 5 minutes, then remove from cookie sheets to wire racks to cool completely.

For the Dip: Melt semisweet and milk chocolates in top of double boiler set over simmering water just until melted. Remove from heat.

Place chopped hazelnuts in a shallow bowl; set aside.

Dip one end of each cookie into melted chocolate, then into hazelnuts. Place on waxed paper and let stand until chocolate is set, about 1 hour. Makes about 2 dozen.

Even before the chocolate has had a chance to set, it's hard to resist doing a quality-control check on these Chocolate-Dipped Shortbread Logs with Hazelnuts.

Hazelnut-Espresso Shortbread Cookies

More shortbread, but this time with an Italian flair!

1 cup unsalted butter, room temperature
1 cup firmly packed light brown sugar
2 cups unbleached, all-purpose flour
3 tbsp. cornstarch
2 tsp. instant espresso powder
¾ tsp. salt
1 tsp. pure vanilla extract
⅔ cup hazelnuts, toasted, skinned, and finely chopped

GLAZE

2 tbsp. unsalted butter, room temperature
1 tsp. instant espresso powder
2 oz. semisweet chocolate, coarsely chopped

BEV'S BITES

Worth repeating: To skin hazelnuts: place hazelnuts on an ungreased jellyroll pan and bake at 325 degrees for 20 to 25 minutes. Immediately dump into a clean kitchen towel, spreading into a single layer. Working quickly, fold half of the towel over hazelnuts and rub continuously back and forth over hazelnuts to remove their skins. Remove skinned hazelnuts to plate to cool.

Heat oven to 350 degrees.

Using an electric mixer, in a large bowl, combine the butter and brown sugar until light and fluffy. Scrape down sides and bottom of bowl.

Mix in the flour, cornstarch, espresso powder, salt, and vanilla just until combined. Do not overbeat. Stir in hazelnuts.

Divide dough in half and shape into 2 disks. Press or roll each half on an ungreased cookie sheet to a 9" circle. Using a pizza cutter or knife, score each round into 12 to 18 wedges.

Bake for 20 to 22 minutes or until a light golden brown. Cool 2 minutes, then cut each shortbread round into 12 to 18 pieces. Remove from cookie sheets to wire racks to cool completely.

For the Glaze: In a small saucepan, combine the remaining butter with the espresso powder; add the chocolate and stir over low heat until chocolate is melted and mixture is combined and smooth. Remove from heat.

Drizzle chocolate mixture over cookie wedges set on a cooling rack atop waxed paper. Let stand until chocolate sets. Makes 2 to 3 dozen.

Brown Sugar with Chips of Chocolate Shortbread Cookies

A rich blend of brown sugar, butter, and chocolate chips come together to make a very satisfying cookie.

1 cup unsalted butter, room temperature
1/2 cup firmly packed light brown sugar
1 tsp. pure vanilla extract
2 cups unbleached, all-purpose flour
1/4 cup cornstarch
1/2 cup finely chopped semisweet chocolate pieces
1/4 cup granulated sugar

BEV'S BITES

It's worth repeating:
So how does the sugar stick to the bottom of the glass? There are two tricks to try: I prefer to brush the bottom of the glass lightly with water, then quickly press into sugar to adhere. Alternately, you can spray (ever so lightly) the bottom of the glass with a vegetable cooking spray, then quickly press into sugar to adhere. Do either of these only as necessary.

Heat oven to 300 degrees.

Using an electric mixer, in a large bowl, beat together the butter and brown sugar until light and fluffy. Scrape down sides and bottom of bowl. Stir in vanilla.

Mix in the flour and cornstarch just until blended, then stir in the chocolate pieces.

Place sugar in a shallow bowl.

Scoop cookie dough into 1" balls and place on ungreased cookie sheets, 1½" apart. Press dough with bottom of a glass dipped in sugar.

Bake for 25 to 30 minutes or just until bottoms of cookies begin to turn light golden in color.

Cool 1 minute, then remove from cookie sheets to wire racks to cool completely. Makes about 3 dozen.

If I hand these Wedges of Shortbread, Double Dipped to the teacher
with my essay does that qualify for extra credit??

Wedges of Shortbread, Double Dipped

A sometimes difficult dough, not for the faint of heart, but well worth the effort!

½ cup granulated sugar
1 cup unsalted butter, cold
1¾ cups unbleached, all-purpose flour
¼ cup semolina flour
⅛ cup plus 1 tbsp. cornstarch
2 tbsp. pure vanilla extract

GLAZE

5 oz. bittersweet chocolate, coarsely
   chopped
5 oz. white chocolate, coarsely chopped

BEV'S BITES

I learned to love the textures and flavors semolina flour imparts when I was in Italy. Semolina flour is more coarsely ground than normal wheat flours, and gives this shortbread a pleasant, grainy flavor and crunch.

Heat oven to 325 degrees.

Using an electric mixer, in a large bowl, beat together the sugar and butter just until combined. Scrape down sides and bottom of bowl.

Add in the unbleached, all-purpose and semolina flours, cornstarch, and vanilla, beating until combined. Form this crumbly mass into a ball and knead lightly.

Divide dough into thirds and form each third into a 5" disk on an ungreased cookie sheet. Score into 8 pieces; prick several times with the tines of a fork.

Bake for 25 to 30 minutes or until light golden in color. Cool 1 minute, then carefully cut through lines to separate wedges of shortbread.

Remove from cookie sheets to wire racks to cool completely.

For the Glaze: In a double boiler, melt the bittersweet chocolate; remove and set aside. In another double boiler or a bowl set over the simmering water, melt the white chocolate; remove and set aside.

Place wire rack over waxed paper. Dip one edge of each cookie in the bittersweet chocolate, then the opposite edge in the white chocolate. Allow chocolate to set. Makes about 2 dozen.

Shortbread with a Touch of Edible Flowers

Each spring, our lawn is filled with unsprayed, organically grown violets. I love to use them in creative ways and this shortbread is no exception.

½ cup unsalted butter, cold
1¼ cups unbleached, all-purpose flour
3 tbsp. granulated sugar

TOPPING

3 tbsp. pasteurized liquid egg whites
20 edible violets
Superfine sugar

BEV'S BITES

Like so many fragile shortbreads, patience is the key . . . and the tasty rewards are many!

Heat oven to 325 degrees.

Using an electric mixer, in a large bowl, beat the butter until softened. Stir in the flour and sugar, mixing just until dough resembles fine crumbs and starts to cling together.

Remove from bowl and form mixture into a ball, kneading lightly until smooth.

Place dough on ungreased cookie sheet and pat into a 9" or 10" circle. Cut circle into 16 to 20 wedges, leaving circle intact.

Bake for 28 to 30 minutes or until edges are a light golden in color and center is set. Cool 1 minute, then recut wedges while still warm.

Cool on cookie sheet on wire rack. Brush tops of wedges with egg whites, top with a violet, and gently brush egg white over violet (being careful not to "glob" it on). Sprinkle with superfine sugar.

Bake for an additional 5 minutes. Cool on wire rack. Makes about 16 to 20 wedges.

Lavender Bud Shortbread Cookies

Dried lavender buds and fresh lemon zest add an elegant twist to a refrigerator cookie.

1½ cups unbleached, all-purpose flour
1 tsp. dried lavender buds, ground with a mortar and pestle
1 tsp. fresh orange zest, finely grated
¼ tsp. salt
¾ cup unsalted butter, room temperature
1 cup confectioners' sugar, sifted

FROSTING

¼ cup unsalted butter, room temperature
1 cup confectioners' sugar, sifted
1 tbsp. milk, whole or 2 percent

BEV'S BITES ———

Dough requires some work to keep it all together to roll into a log . . . it's crumbly. However, the dough's texture is what helps make for a crisp, buttery cookie.

Stir together the flour, lavender buds, orange zest, and salt in a medium bowl; set aside.

Using an electric mixer, in a large bowl, beat the butter and confectioners' sugar until combined. Scrape down sides and bottom of bowl.

Add the flour mixture; beat until combined.

Shape dough into a 10" long log; wrap in plastic wrap. Chill dough for 2 hours or until firm.

Heat oven to 375 degrees. Cut roll into ¼" thick slices, placing slices 2" apart on ungreased cookie sheets. Bake for 12 to 15 minutes or until edges just begin to turn a light golden brown.

Cool 1 minute, then remove from cookie sheets to wire racks to cool completely.

For the Frosting: In a small bowl, combine the butter, confectioners' sugar, and milk. Whisk until smooth, stirring in additional milk if necessary to reach desired spreading consistency. Spread Frosting on cooled cookies. Makes about 2½ dozen.

Candied-Ginger Shortbread

Candied ginger adds a sweet tang to this tender, buttery shortbread recipe.

1 cup unsalted butter, room temperature
$\frac{1}{2}$ cup firmly packed light brown sugar
$\frac{1}{2}$ tsp. ground ginger
2 cups unbleached, all-purpose flour
$\frac{1}{4}$ tsp. salt
$\frac{1}{4}$ tsp. pure vanilla extract
$\frac{1}{2}$ cup candied ginger, finely chopped

BEV'S BITES

Candied ginger (or crystallized ginger) is fresh ginger that has been cooked in a sugar syrup and coated with coarse sugar.

Using an electric mixer, in a large bowl, beat together the butter and brown sugar until light and fluffy. Scrape down sides and bottom of bowl.

Add the ground ginger, flour, and salt, beating just until combined. Do not overmix.

Stir in the vanilla and chopped candied ginger.

Divide dough in half and shape into 2 disks. Wrap in plastic wrap; flatten to $\frac{1}{4}$". Chill dough for 2 hours.

Heat oven to 300 degrees. Turn dough out, one disk at a time (keeping remaining dough refrigerated), on a lightly floured surface. Cut with your favorite 2" cookie cutters (scalloped ovals or heart-shaped cutters make for attractive shapes).

Arrange cookies 2" apart on ungreased cookie sheets. Bake for 20 minutes or just until they begin to turn light golden in color.

Cool 1 minute, then remove from cookie sheets to wire racks to cool completely. Makes about $2\frac{1}{2}$ dozen.

Mascarpone Sandwich Cookies

These cookies are sinfully rich . . . and a show-stopper on a cookie tray.

½ cup unsalted butter, room temperature
1 cup granulated sugar
1 tsp. baking powder
½ tsp. freshly grated nutmeg
¼ tsp. baking soda
¼ tsp. salt
½ cup mascarpone cheese
1 large egg
2½ cups unbleached, all-purpose flour

GLAZE AND FILLING

1 cup confectioners' sugar, sifted
¼ tsp. pure vanilla extract
2 to 4 tsp. milk, whole or 2 percent
1 cup seedless raspberry preserves or
  apricot fruit spread

BEV'S BITES

What is mascarpone? It's a buttery rich, soft double (or sometimes triple) cream cheese, originally hailing from Italy.

These cookies are also amazing using your favorite ganache recipe in place of the preserves.

Using an electric mixer, in a large mixing bowl, beat together the butter and sugar until light and fluffy. Scrape sides and bottom of bowl.

Add the baking powder, nutmeg, baking soda, and salt. Stir to blend.

Beat in mascarpone cheese and egg. Scrape sides and bottom of bowl.

Mix in flour until blended.

Divide dough in half and shape into 2 disks. Wrap in plastic wrap; flatten to ½". Chill dough for 2 hours.

Heat oven to 375 degrees. Roll dough out on a lightly floured surface to ⅛" thick, one disk at a time (keeping remaining dough refrigerated).

Using 3" round cookie cutters, cut out dough. Cut a small shape from the centers of half of the cookies.

Place whole cookies on parchment-paper-lined cookie sheets and the cutout cookies on another parchment-paper-lined cookie sheet. (These two types will probably bake at different rates.)

Bake for 5 to 8 minutes or until edges just begin to turn a light golden brown. Cool 1 minute, then remove from cookie sheets to wire racks to cool completely.

For the Glaze: In a small bowl, whisk together the confectioners' sugar and vanilla with enough milk to make a smooth spreadable glaze. Spread the cutout cookies with Glaze; let Glaze set.

When ready to assemble, spread the flat side of each whole cookie with about ½ tsp. of preserves or fruit spread. Top with a glazed cutout cookie, flat side down. Makes about 3 dozen.

Sour Cream Lemon Drops

A soft, tender cookie bursting with the fresh flavors of a lemon drop.

1 cup granulated sugar
½ cup unsalted butter, room temperature
½ cup sour cream, room temperature
2 large eggs
2 tsp. fresh lemon zest, finely grated
¾ tsp. pure lemon juice
2½ cups unbleached, all-purpose flour
1 tsp. baking powder
½ tsp. salt

GLAZE

1 cup confectioners' sugar, sifted
1 tsp. lemon zest
1 to 2 tbsp. fresh lemon juice

Heat oven to 350 degrees.

Using an electric mixer, in a large bowl, combine the sugar and butter, beating until creamy. Scrape down sides and bottom of bowl.

Add sour cream, eggs, zest, and lemon juice and continue to beat until well mixed.

Mix in the flour, baking powder, and salt on low speed just until combined. Scrape down sides and bottom of bowl.

Drop dough by rounded teaspoonfuls 1½" apart on parchment-paper-lined cookie sheets. Bake for 10 to 13 minutes or just until cookies are light golden brown.

Cool 1 minute, then remove from cookie sheets to wire racks to cool completely.

For the Glaze: In a small bowl, whisk together the confectioners' sugar, zest, and enough lemon juice for desired glazing consistency. Frost cooled cookies. Makes about 2½ dozen.

Mexican Wedding Cookies with a Twist

Not a cake at all, these classic cookies get a new twist from my love of pistachios and dried cherries. Created for a holiday cookies class, these tender bites are always a hit.

2 cups unsalted butter, room temperature
1 cup confectioners' sugar, sifted, plus additional for coating cookies
2 tbsp. pure vanilla extract
1 tsp. salt
$^3/_4$ cup salted and roasted natural pistachios, finely chopped
$^3/_4$ cup tart dried cherries, snipped into pieces
$2^1/_2$ cups cake flour, sifted
$2^2/_3$ cups unbleached, all-purpose flour

BEV'S BITES

The addition of cake flour, with its lack of gluten, helps make these cookies extra tender. Make sure to sift it after measuring to remove any lumps.

Heat oven to 350 degrees. Line cookies sheets with parchment paper.

Using an electric mixer, in a large bowl, beat the butter and confectioners' sugar until light and fluffy. Scrape sides and bottom of bowl.

Mix in the vanilla and salt, then the pistachios and dried cherries.

Stir in the cake and unbleached, all-purpose flours, mixing just until blended. Do not overmix.

Shape dough by generous tablespoonfuls into balls. Place on prepared cookie sheets, spacing 1" apart.

Bake until bottoms of cookies just begin to turn a light golden brown, about 12 to 14 minutes.

Cool 5 minutes, then roll in confectioners' sugar. Remove to wire racks to cool completely. Reroll in confectioners' sugar. Makes about 3 dozen.

Baby Black and Whites

A flavorful cookie coated with a white glaze and a dark glaze . . . the perfect way to add bite-size variety to a cookie tray.

³/₄ cup granulated sugar
¹/₂ cup unsalted butter, room temperature
1 large egg
1¹/₂ cups unbleached, all-purpose flour
1 tsp. cream of tartar
¹/₂ tsp. baking soda
¹/₂ tsp. pure vanilla extract

GLAZE

2¹/₂ cups confectioners' sugar, sifted
1 tbsp. unsalted butter, room temperature
2 tbsp. brown rice syrup
3 to 4 tbsp. milk, whole or 2 percent
1 oz. bittersweet chocolate, melted and cooled

BEV'S BITES

Brown rice syrup is a naturally sweetened syrup (and a great substitute for corn syrup). It is a mildly sweet, caramel-flavored, golden syrup made from rice. You should find it at specialty grocery stores, natural food stores, and health food stores.

Heat oven to 400 degrees. Using an electric mixer, in a large bowl, combine the sugar, butter, and egg, beating until creamy. Scrape down sides and bottom of bowl.

With mixer on low, add the flour, cream of tartar, baking soda, and vanilla. Beat until well mixed. Scrape down sides and bottom of bowl.

Shape rounded teaspoonfuls of dough into 1" balls. Place 1¹/₂" apart on ungreased cookie sheets. Bake for 6 to 8 minutes or until edges just begin to turn a light golden brown.

Cool 1 minute, then remove from cookie sheets to wire racks to cool completely.

For the Glaze: Using an electric mixer, in a medium bowl, beat together the confectioners' sugar, butter, and rice syrup, adding just enough milk for desired glazing consistency. Remove 1 cup of the Glaze to a small bowl and whisk in the melted chocolate.

Brush half of each cookie with White Glaze; let stand until set (about 15 minutes). Then brush other half with Chocolate Glaze. (If Chocolate Glaze begins to harden, heat slightly over low heat, whisking to soften.)

Allow cookies to set atop waxed paper. Makes about 3 dozen.

Much Better Than Fruitcake Bars

Honestly, I hate fruitcake . . . but a collection of quality dried fruits, soaked in brandy in a brown-sugar-laced bar is hard to resist!

1 cup unsalted butter, room temperature plus additional, melted, for brushing foil
1 cup brandy
1 cup seedless raisins
1 cup dried apricots, snipped into pieces
1 cup dried cranberries
1 cup pitted dates, snipped into pieces
1 cup dried cherries, snipped into pieces
1 cup firmly packed light brown sugar
1 cup firmly packed dark brown sugar
3 large eggs
1 tsp. pure vanilla extract
2 cups unbleached, all-purpose flour, divided
½ tsp. salt

Heat oven to 350 degrees. Line a 13x9" baking pan with foil; gently brush foil with melted butter; set aside.

Heat the brandy to a simmer in a medium saucepan. Toss in the raisins, apricots, cranberries, dates, and cherries; cover. Remove from heat and let dried fruits absorb some of the brandy, about 1 hour.

Using an electric mixer, in a large bowl, beat together the butter and brown sugar until light and fluffy. Scrape sides and bottom of bowl.

Add eggs and vanilla, beating until well blended. Mix in 1 cup of the flour and the salt, stirring just until blended.

Remove the soaked fruit mixture (with any remaining liquid) to a medium bowl. Toss the remaining 1 cup of flour with the dried fruit mixture, tossing gently until combined.

Add this mixture to the bar batter, then spoon into prepared pan.

Bake for 35 to 45 minutes or just until a toothpick or cake tester inserted in center comes out clean. Cool 1 hour in pan, then, using foil to gently lift out of pan, transfer to a wire rack to cool completely.

When cool, invert and peel off foil, then flip upright onto a cutting board. Cut into 36 bars.

Ginger Chewy

Fellow chef Heather Haviland, owner of Sweet Mosaic Inc. and Lucky's Café in Cleveland, was kind enough to share the recipe for this delightful cookie. It's a mainstay in her café, and when they run out, she says, "Our customers act like I just canceled Christmas!"

3¼ cups unbleached, all-purpose flour
1½ tsp. baking soda
1¼ tsp. ground ginger
1¼ tsp. ground cinnamon
1¼ tsp. ground cloves
½ cup unsalted butter, room temperature
1 tsp. kosher salt
1 cup firmly packed light brown sugar
2 large eggs
⅓ cup blackstrap molasses, unsulphured
Granulated sugar for rolling

BEV'S BITES

If you visit Lucky's Café, you'll notice that they make these large, so feel free to scoop a tbsp. size instead, adjusting baking time accordingly.

Heather uses kosher salt for her cookies, but you can substitute sea salt or other salt with good results. Kosher salt intensifies the flavors.

Heat oven to 325 degrees. Line cookie sheets with parchment paper. In a medium bowl, sift together the flour, baking soda, ginger, cinnamon, and cloves; set aside.

Using an electric mixer, in a large bowl, beat the butter, salt, and brown sugar on medium-high speed until light and fluffy. Scrape down sides and bottom of bowl.

Add eggs, mixing to combine. Scrape down sides and bottom of bowl, then add the molasses, mixing to combine.

Add the flour mixture and stir until combined. Do not overmix.

Use a tsp. to make small balls of dough. Roll dough into granulated sugar and place on prepared cookie sheets, allowing enough room for the cookies to double in size while they bake.

Bake for 15 to 17 minutes. Cookies will be slightly soft in the middle when done. Cool 1 minute, then remove from cookie sheets to wire racks to cool completely. Makes about 5 dozen.

"Open Sesame" Cookies

A cookie with a deep nutty flavor, perfect served with a Middle Eastern lunch!

½ cup firmly packed light brown sugar
½ cup firmly packed dark brown sugar
⅓ cup tahini
2 tbsp. toasted sesame oil
1 tbsp. light corn syrup or brown rice
   syrup
2 tsp. pure vanilla extract
1 large egg
1½ cups unbleached, all-purpose flour
1½ tbsp. cornstarch or arrowroot
1 tsp. baking powder
½ tsp. baking soda
¼ tsp. salt
½ cup granulated sugar

BEV'S BITES

Tahini is a thick paste made of ground sesame seeds.

Arrowroot, a starchy byproduct of a tropical tuber, is used as a thickening agent. It's absolutely tasteless and becomes clear when cooked.

Heat oven to 375 degrees.

Using an electric mixer, in a large bowl, combine the light and dark brown sugars, tahini, oil, and syrup, beating until light and well blended.

Add the vanilla and egg, stirring until blended. Mix in the flour, cornstarch, baking powder, baking soda, and salt just until blended. Do not overbeat.

Shape dough into 1" balls and place 2" apart on ungreased cookie sheets. Press dough with bottom of a glass dipped in granulated sugar.

Bake for 8 to 10 minutes or just until cookies are a light golden brown. Cool 1 minute, then remove from cookie sheets to wire racks to cool completely. Makes about 2½ dozen.

These PB&Js are a brown bagger's lunch-time delight.

PB&Js

The perfect cookie to take to lunch . . . featuring peanut butter and your favorite jelly!

¾ cup firmly packed light brown sugar
⅔ cup granulated sugar
½ cup smooth peanut butter
¼ cup unsalted butter, softened
2 large eggs
1 tsp. pure vanilla extract
2 cups unbleached, all-purpose flour
⅛ cup finely ground, shelled, roasted
    and salted peanuts
¼ tsp. salt

FILLING

½ cup grape jelly or your favorite
1 tsp. fresh lemon juice

Using an electric mixer, in a large bowl, combine the sugars, peanut butter, and butter and beat until light and fluffy. Scrape down sides and bottom of bowl.

Add the eggs and vanilla, beating until well blended.

Mix in flour, peanuts, and salt, stirring just until combined. Do not overbeat. Cover and chill dough for 2 hours.

Heat oven to 350 degrees. Line cookie sheets with parchment paper.

Shape dough into balls, about tbsp. size each, and place 1½" apart on prepared cookie sheets. Press thumb indentation into center of each dough ball.

Bake cookies for 10 to 14 minutes or until a light golden brown in color. Cool 1 minute, then remove from cookie sheets to wire racks to cool completely.

For the Filling: In a small bowl, beat together the jelly and lemon juice until well blended. Spoon about ½ tsp. of mixture into the center of each cookie. Makes about 2½ dozen.

Just the Flax, Ma'am

A crunchy cookie with the added health benefits of flax meal, this cookie is one of my favorites to munch on.

1 cup unsalted butter, room temperature
¾ cup granulated sugar
1 cup firmly packed light brown sugar
¼ cup firmly packed dark brown sugar
2 large eggs
1 tsp. pure vanilla extract
2 cups unbleached, all-purpose flour
1 cup old-fashioned rolled oats (not quick cooking)
½ cup flaxseed meal
½ tsp. salt
1 tsp. baking powder
1 tsp. baking soda
1½ cups almonds, lightly toasted then finely chopped

BEV'S BITES

Flaxseed has a mild, nutty flavor, and this tiny seed, ground into a meal, is a rich source of Omega-3 fatty acids, calcium, iron, niacin, phosphorous, and vitamin E. Store your flax in the refrigerator or freezer.

Heat oven to 350 degrees.

Using an electric mixer, in a large bowl, beat the butter and sugars until light and fluffy.

Beat in eggs and vanilla, mixing well. Scrape down sides and bottom of bowl.

Add the flour, oats, flaxseed meal, salt, baking powder, and baking soda; mix until combined.

Stir in the almonds until blended.

Drop by rounded tablespoonfuls on ungreased cookie sheets, leaving about 1½" between as cookies will spread during baking.

Bake for 9 to 10 minutes or just until cookies begin to turn a light golden brown on top. Cool 1 minute, then remove from cookie sheets to wire racks to cool completely. Makes about 4½ dozen.

REFRIGERATOR COOKIES AND BAR COOKIES

These Lemon Wafer Crunch are fun to eat from the outside in—a coarse, sugary crunch of an edge followed by a burst of lemon center!

Refrigerator Cookies

These slice-and-bake cookies are formed by shaping dough into a cylinder, chilling until firm, and slicing into thin disks before baking. Perfect for stashing in the freezer or refrigerator for spur-of-the-moment cookies (oh, don't you just love those moments!).

A helpful hint or two:

* When shaping dough into a cylinder or log, it helps to roll it back and forth across a lightly floured surface.

* The firmer the dough, the easier to slice.

* A thin serrated knife or a very sharp, thin-bladed knife makes nice clean slices.

* After every three cuts, roll the cylinder a quarter turn to help retain its round shape.

When I was younger, these were called icebox cookies. Does anyone know what an icebox is anymore?

Bar Cookies

A busy baker's salvation. Mix up a batch, bake it in a pan, cut it into squares, and you're satisfied without sacrificing flavor.

A helpful hint or two:

* Size matters. Use the right size pan. Not sure about the size? Measure it across the top from one edge to the other. Baking times and textures are dependent on the right size pan.

* For easier removal, I often line the pan with foil then brush lightly with melted butter (to prevent tears in the foil).

* Aromas make warm bar cookies hard to resist, but if you cut them before they're cool, you'll smash them!

It's time to step up to the bar . . . and remember, the most difficult part of baking these two types of cookies may be resisting the urge to eat them all before you share!

Lemon Wafer Crunch

Loaded with lemon flavor and the crunch of coarse sugar, these decidedly lemon crunch cookies will become favorites.

½ cup plus 2 tbsp. unsalted butter, room temperature
½ cup plus 3 tbsp. granulated sugar
1 tsp. pure vanilla extract
2 tbsp. loosely packed, fresh lemon zest, finely grated
¼ cup fresh lemon juice
1½ cups unbleached, all-purpose flour
½ tsp. baking powder
¼ tsp. baking soda
¼ tsp. salt
Coarse sugar

BEV'S BITES

When buying citrus fruit, such as lemons, buy them for their weight as well as appearance. If the fruit is heavy, it will yield a thin but substantial skin and lots of fruit inside.

Using an electric mixer, in a large bowl, cream together the butter and sugar until light and fluffy. Scrape down sides and bottom of bowl.

Blend in the vanilla, zest, and juice, stopping once to scrape down sides and bottom of bowl. Mixture will look curdled.

Add the flour, baking powder, baking soda, and salt, mixing until blended.

On a lightly floured surface, shape the dough into an 8" long log and roll in plastic wrap or waxed paper. Twist the ends to seal the cylinder of dough.

Chill dough for 2 hours up to overnight.

When ready to bake, heat the oven to 350 degrees. Line cookie sheets with parchment paper.

Remove the dough from the refrigerator, unwrap it, and roll the cylinder in the coarse sugar, pressing gently so sugar crystals adhere and rocking cylinder back and forth to keep its rounded shape.

Cut into ¼" thick slices and place 1" apart on prepared cookie sheets.

Bake for 10 to 14 minutes or just until they are a light golden around edges.

Cool 1 minute, then remove from cookie sheets to wire racks to cool completely. Makes about 2½ dozen.

These Tart-Topped Lemon Cookies are all lined up and ready to eat.

Tart-Topped Lemon Cookies

This cookie's title says it all: It's bursting with pure citrus flavors and is perfect with a cup of tea or some fresh summer fruits.

2 cups plus 2 tbsp. cake flour, sifted
¼ tsp. baking powder
½ tsp. salt
1 tbsp. fresh lemon zest, finely grated
1 tsp. pure vanilla extract
2 tbsp. fresh lemon juice
¾ cup unsalted butter, room temperature
1 cup confectioners' sugar, sifted
2½ tsp. milk, whole or 2 percent

TOPPING

1 tsp. fresh lemon zest, finely grated
⅓ cup confectioners' sugar, sifted
1 tbsp. fresh lemon juice
1 to 2 tbsp. milk, whole or 2 percent

BEV'S BITES

No cake flour? For a cookie that's just as flavorful but not quite as tender, use 2 cups of unbleached, all-purpose flour in place of the cake flour.

Using an electric mixer, in a large bowl, combine the flour, baking powder, salt, and lemon zest, stirring to blend.

Stir in the vanilla and lemon juice. Add the butter and confectioners' sugar and mix until the dough just comes together. Divide dough in half.

Shape each half of dough into an 8" log and roll on a long sheet of waxed paper or plastic wrap. Twist the ends to seal the cylinders of dough. Chill the dough for 4 hours up to overnight.

Heat oven to 325 degrees. Line cookie sheets with parchment paper.

Unwrap 1 log at a time and cut into ¼" thick slices, placing 2" apart on prepared cookie sheets.

Bake 20 to 28 minutes, until the centers are set and the edges are light golden. Cool 1 minute, then remove from cookie sheets to wire racks to cool completely.

For the Topping: In a small bowl, whisk together the zest, confectioners' sugar, and lemon juice, adding just enough milk to make a spoonable glaze.

Place cooling racks over waxed paper and spoon some topping over each cookie. Allow to set. Makes about 2½ dozen.

Lemon Sugar Cookies

You can often catch me sprinkling some of the extra lemon sugar atop fresh berries!

½ cup unsalted butter, room temperature
1 cup granulated sugar
½ cup Lemon Sugar, divided
1 large egg
1 tsp. pure vanilla extract
1¼ cups unbleached, all-purpose flour
1 tsp. baking powder
½ tsp. salt

BEV'S BITES

Lemon Sugar is easy to make: Remove the zest from 4 to 6 large lemons (about ½ cup finely grated). Combine the zest with 2¼ cups granulated sugar in a food processor. Pulse until mixture is pale yellow with bits of zest still visible. Keep any remaining Lemon Sugar in an airtight container in the refrigerator.

Stir a spoonful into your tea for a tasty treat!

Using an electric mixer, in a large bowl, beat together the butter, sugar, and 2 tbsp. of the Lemon Sugar until light and fluffy. Scrape down sides and bottom of bowl.

Beat in the egg and vanilla, mixing until blended. Mix in the flour, baking powder, and salt just until combined.

On a lightly floured surface, form dough into a 10" log. Wrap in plastic wrap or waxed paper. Twist the ends to seal the cylinder of dough.

Chill dough for 4 hours up to overnight.

Heat oven to 375 degrees. Remove wrapper and cut each log into ¼" thick slices, spacing ½" apart on ungreased cookie sheets. Bake for 10 to 12 minutes or just until a light golden color.

Transfer to a cooling rack set over waxed paper. Sprinkle tops with remaining Lemon Sugar. Cool completely on wire racks. Makes about 2½ dozen.

Orange Crisps

Just a thin wafer? One more of these will hardly be enough.

1 cup unsalted butter, room temperature
½ cup firmly packed light brown sugar
½ cup granulated sugar
¼ cup fresh orange zest, finely grated
1 large egg
2 tbsp. frozen orange juice concentrate, thawed
2¼ cups unbleached, all-purpose flour
¼ tsp. baking soda
½ tsp. salt

BEV'S BITES

This refrigerator cookie is loaded with fresh orange zest, so a sharp zester/grater, such as a Microplane®, will become your new best friend.

Using an electric mixer, in a large bowl, cream together the butter, sugars, and zest until light and fluffy. Scrape down sides and bottom of bowl.

Add the egg and orange juice concentrate, beating until blended. Scrape down sides and bottom of bowl.

Stir in the flour, baking soda, and salt just until blended.

Shape the dough into a 12" log and roll on a long sheet of waxed paper or plastic wrap. Twist the ends to seal the cylinder of dough. Chill the dough for 4 hours up to overnight.

Heat the oven to 400 degrees. Line cookie sheets with parchment paper.

Unwrap log and cut into ⅛" thick slices, placing 1½" apart on prepared cookie sheets.

Bake for 5 to 7 minutes or just until they are firm to the touch and golden around the edges. Cool on baking sheets atop wire racks. Makes about 5 dozen.

Mocha Pinwheels

Chocolate, orange, and espresso, all swirled together, make for a great cookie combination.

1 oz. bittersweet chocolate, coarsely chopped
½ cup granulated sugar
½ cup unsalted butter, room temperature
1 large egg
1 tsp. pure vanilla extract
1½ cups unbleached, all-purpose flour
½ tsp. baking powder
¼ tsp. salt
1 tsp. instant espresso powder
1½ tsp. fresh orange zest, finely grated

Melt chocolate in a double boiler set over just simmering water, stirring until smooth. Remove from heat to cool.

Using an electric mixer, in a large bowl, beat together the sugar, butter, egg, and vanilla until light and creamy. Scrape down sides and bottom of bowl.

With mixer on low speed, stir in the flour, baking powder, and salt until mixed.

In a medium bowl, combine the melted chocolate with espresso powder, stirring to blend. Add half of the dough to this mixture, beating until well mixed.

Add the orange zest to the remaining plain dough, beating until well mixed.

Shape each half into a 4x5" rectangle. Wrap in plastic wrap or waxed paper and refrigerate for 1½ hours.

Roll out chocolate dough between 2 sheets of lightly floured waxed paper until it reaches the shape of a 12x7" rectangle. Repeat with orange zest dough.

Place orange zest dough atop the chocolate dough, gently pressing doughs together.

Roll up, jellyroll fashion, starting with the 12" side.

Wrap in plastic wrap or waxed paper. Twist the ends to seal the cylinder of dough. Refrigerate until firm, at least 2 hours up to overnight.

Heat oven to 375 degrees. Unwrap and cut roll with sharp knife into ¼" slices, placing 1" apart on ungreased cookie sheets. Bake for 8 to 9 minutes or just until set.

Cool 1 minute, then remove from cookie sheets to wire racks to cool completely. Makes about 2½ dozen.

Two Mocha Pinwheels with a hint of mischief.
Don't gaze directly into the cookies!

No-Bake Truffle Cookies

An elegant no-bake cookie, perfect for something sophisticated after a special meal. I often do these for chocolate demonstrations and classes during the holidays, and people are always amazed at how decadent they are.

11 oz. mandarin orange segments, drained
6 oz. bittersweet chocolate, finely chopped
¼ cup heavy (whipping) cream
3 tbsp. unsalted butter, room temperature
3 cups crushed vanilla wafers or chocolate wafers
½ cup confectioners' sugar, sifted
½ cup ground pecans
2 tbsp. Grand Marnier or orange juice concentrate, thawed
1 cup chocolate sprinkles

BEV'S BITES
Toast and cool the pecans before grinding to bring out their flavor.

In a food processor, chop drained mandarin oranges until very fine.

In a medium saucepan, combine the oranges, chocolate pieces, cream, and butter and heat over low heat until chocolate melts, watching closely and stirring constantly.

Once chocolate melts, cook 3 additional minutes, stirring occasionally. Remove from heat and stir in cookie crumbs, confectioners' sugar, pecans, and Grand Marnier or juice concentrate.

Cover and chill dough for 1 hour or until mixture is firm enough to handle.

Shape into 1" balls, rolling each in the chocolate sprinkles. Keep refrigerated until ready to serve. Makes about 3 dozen.

Crisp Oatmeal Slice and Bakes

A thin, crisp slice-and-bake cookie, perfect for one of those spur-of-the-homemade-cookie moments—subtle flavors and lots of crunch!

½ cup unsalted butter, room temperature
½ cup shortening
½ cup firmly packed light brown sugar
½ cup firmly packed dark brown sugar
2 large eggs
1 tsp. pure vanilla extract
2 cups quick-cooking oats
1½ cups unbleached, all-purpose flour
1 tsp. baking soda
¼ tsp. salt
1 cup seedless raisins, snipped into pieces

Using an electric mixer, in a large bowl, combine the butter, shortening, and light and dark brown sugars until light and creamy. Scrape down sides and bottom of bowl.

Add eggs and vanilla, beating until well blended. Stir in oats, flour, baking soda, salt, and raisins just until combined. Do not overbeat.

Shape mixture into 2 6" logs. Wrap in plastic wrap or waxed paper. Twist the ends to seal the cylinders of dough. Chill dough for 2 hours up to overnight.

Heat oven to 350 degrees. Unwrap logs and cut rolls quickly into ¼" thick slices using a large, sharp knife. Space 1" apart on ungreased cookie sheets.

Bake for 13 to 15 minutes or just until light golden brown.

Cool 1 minute, then remove from cookie sheets to wire racks to cool completely. Makes about 2½ dozen.

John's Butterscotch Rectangles

A favorite at our home, John will often make these with the addition of finely ground toasted walnuts or pecans added to the dough. Sometimes he even shares a cookie or two with me!

1 cup granulated sugar
1 cup firmly packed light brown sugar
1½ cups unsalted butter, room temperature
3 large eggs
4½ cups unbleached, all-purpose flour
2 tsp. baking powder
1 tsp. baking soda
1 tsp. ground cinnamon
½ tsp. salt

BEV'S BITES
Loaf pans may be omitted and dough can be shaped into 2 long logs. Wrap in plastic wrap or waxed paper. Freeze for 2 to 3 hours or until well chilled.

Using an electric mixer, in a large bowl, beat together the sugars and butter until light and fluffy. Scrape down sides and bottom of bowl.

Add eggs, blending well. Stir in the flour, baking powder, baking soda, cinnamon, and salt; mix well until combined.

For rectangular cookies, line 2 8x4" loaf pans with foil, allowing foil to extend over edge of pan. Press half of the dough into each pan, then fold foil to seal. Freeze for 2 to 3 hours or until well chilled.

Heat oven to 350 degrees. Line cookie sheets with parchment paper. Unfold foil (one batch at a time); lift dough from pan.

Remove foil, then cut dough into ¼" thick slices, placing 2" apart on prepared cookie sheets.

Bake for 9 to 13 minutes or just until a light golden brown.

Cool 1 minute, then remove from cookie sheets to wire racks to cool completely. Makes about 4 dozen.

Cinnamon Sugar-Topped Anise Crisps

A change of pace, licorice-scented cookie that will be the center of conversation at your next dessert party.

1¹⁄₃ cups unbleached, all-purpose flour
1 tbsp. cornstarch
1 tsp. ground cinnamon
1 tsp. baking powder
¹⁄₂ tsp. anise seed, crushed
¹⁄₄ tsp. salt
³⁄₄ cup granulated sugar
¹⁄₄ cup unsalted butter, room temperature
1 tbsp. fresh orange juice
1 tsp. pure vanilla extract
1 large egg

TOPPING

1¹⁄₂ tsp. granulated sugar
¹⁄₄ tsp. ground cinnamon

BEV'S BITES

For a thinner, crisper cookie slice logs into ¹⁄₄" thick slices and bake for less time.

Both the leaves and the seed of the anise plant have a distinctive, sweet licorice flavor.

In a medium bowl, combine the flour, cornstarch, cinnamon, baking powder, anise seed, and salt. Set aside.

Using an electric mixer, in a large bowl, beat together the sugar and butter until light and fluffy. Scrape down sides and bottom of bowl.

Add the juice, vanilla, and egg; beat until combined. Scrape down sides and bottom of bowl.

Mix in the flour mixture just until blended. Divide dough in half.

Shape each half of dough into a 6" log and roll on a long sheet of waxed paper or plastic wrap. Twist the ends to seal the cylinders of dough. Chill the dough for 4 hours up to overnight.

Heat oven to 350 degrees. Line cookie sheets with parchment paper.

Unwrap one log at a time and cut into ¹⁄₂" thick slices, placing 2" apart on prepared cookie sheets.

For the Topping: In a small bowl, combine the sugar with the cinnamon and sprinkle evenly over dough slices. Bake for 8 to 10 minutes or until a light golden color.

Cool 1 minute, then remove from cookie sheets to wire racks to cool completely. Makes 2 dozen.

Shortbread Textured Peanut Butter Refrigerator Cookies

An easy-to-make peanut butter cookie with a light, peanutty taste. Slathering some grape jelly on these might just make the perfect late-night snack!

¾ cup unsalted butter, room temperature
8 tbsp. creamy peanut butter
6 tbsp. confectioners' sugar, sifted
6 tbsp. firmly packed light brown sugar
¾ tsp. pure vanilla extract
1 large egg
1¾ cups plus 2 tbsp. unbleached, all-purpose flour
⅛ tsp. baking powder
½ tsp. salt

Using an electric mixer, in a large bowl, cream together the butter, peanut butter, sugars, and vanilla until light and fluffy. Scrape down sides and bottom of bowl.

Mix in the egg until well blended. Scrape down sides and bottom of bowl.

Stir in the flour, baking powder, and salt just until blended. Divide the dough in half.

Shape each half of dough into a 10" log and roll on a long sheet of waxed paper or plastic wrap. Twist the ends to seal the cylinders of dough. Chill the dough for 4 hours up to overnight.

Heat oven to 325 degrees. Line cookie sheets with parchment paper.

Unwrap one log at a time and cut into ¼" thick slices, placing 1" apart on prepared cookie sheets.

Bake until they are a light golden and crisp, about 12 to 15 minutes. Cool 1 minute, then remove from cookie sheets to wire racks to cool completely. Makes about 4 dozen.

Tastes Like Chai Crunch Cookies

If someone wants to share these delightful crunchy cookies, are you obligated to share your cup of tea?!

¾ cup confectioners' sugar, sifted
10 tbsp. unsalted butter, room temperature
1½ cups unbleached, all-purpose flour
⅛ tsp. salt
¼ tsp. ground cinnamon
¼ tsp. ground cardamom
Dash of ground cloves
Dash of freshly ground black pepper

BEV'S BITES ————
Dough takes a bit of work to form logs but persevere!

Chai is often referred to as a beverage made by brewing tea with a mixture of aromatic spices. By itself, chai is merely the generic word for tea in India, Iran, and much of the world.

Using an electric mixer, in a large bowl, beat the sugar and butter until light and fluffy. Scrape down sides and bottom of bowl.

Mix in the flour, salt, cinnamon, cardamom, cloves, and pepper, just until blended. Scrape down sides and bottom of bowl.

Lightly mix in 2 tbsp. of ice water to form a dough. Divide dough in half.

Shape each half of dough into a 6" log and roll on a long sheet of waxed paper or plastic wrap. Twist the ends to seal the cylinders of dough. Chill the dough for 2 hours up to overnight.

Heat oven to 375 degrees. Line cookie sheets with parchment paper.

Unwrap one log at a time and cut into ⅓" thick slices, placing 2" apart on prepared cookie sheets.

Bake for 10 to 12 minutes. Cool 1 minute, then remove from cookie sheets to wire racks to cool completely. Makes about 2½ dozen.

Brownies In The Round

For a rich brownie flavor, slice these cookies ¾" thick.

1 cup unsalted butter, room temperature
1½ cups granulated sugar
6 oz. bittersweet chocolate, melted and cooled
1 large egg
1 tsp. pure vanilla extract
2½ cups unbleached, all-purpose flour
1¼ tsp. baking powder
¼ tsp. baking soda
¼ tsp. salt
4 oz. semisweet chocolate, finely chopped

BEV'S BITES

Remove only one roll at a time from the refrigerator to ease slicing and help maintain shape and texture.

Using an electric mixer, in a large bowl, beat together the butter and sugar until light and fluffy.

Add the melted chocolate, egg, and vanilla and continue to beat until combined. Scrape down sides and bottom of bowl.

Mix in the flour, baking powder, baking soda, and salt, beating until combined. Stir in chopped chocolate pieces.

Divide dough in half and shape each into a 12" long cylinder. Wrap in plastic wrap or waxed paper. Twist the ends to seal the cylinder of dough.

Refrigerate until firm, at least 2 hours up to overnight.

Heat oven to 375 degrees. Cut rolls into ¾" slices and place them 1" apart onto ungreased cookie sheets.

Bake for 7 to 9 minutes or just until set. Cool 1 minute, then remove from cookie sheets to wire racks to cool completely. Makes about 4½ dozen.

Zebra's Envy-Striped Cookies

A little bit of effort yields a beautifully striped cookie that would be the envy of any zebra!

VANILLA DOUGH

½ cup confectioners' sugar, sifted
¼ cup unsalted butter, room temperature
1 large egg yolk
1½ tsp. pure vanilla extract
1¼ cups unbleached, all-purpose flour
⅛ tsp. salt
2 tbsp. ice water

CHOCOLATE DOUGH

1 cup confectioners' sugar, sifted
¼ cup unsalted butter, room temperature
1 large egg yolk
½ tsp. pure vanilla extract
¾ cup unbleached, all-purpose flour
⅓ cup unsweetened cocoa powder, sifted
⅛ tsp. salt
2 tbsp. ice water

BEV'S BITES ————————

This recipe looks (and sounds) a lot more complicated than it really is.

I know, I know . . . overlap this and wrap that. The steps I developed are thorough, having used and taught with these instructions many times in hands-on cookie classes.

Just to ensure ease of use, I gave this recipe to one of my testers who commented, "Recipe worked perfectly!" You'll enjoy the end result if you take a little time to make the dough.

For the Vanilla Dough: Using an electric mixer, in a large bowl, beat together the sugar, butter, and egg yolk until smooth. Add in the vanilla. Scrape down sides and bottom of bowl.

Mix in the flour and salt, beating just until combined. Then add 2 tbsp. of ice water, beating just until moistened. The dough will be slightly crumbly, but do not overmix.

Press dough into a 4" disk. Wrap in plastic wrap and chill for 2 hours or until firm.

For the Chocolate Dough: Using an electric mixer, in a large bowl, beat together the sugar, butter, and egg yolk until smooth. Add in the vanilla. Scrape down sides and bottom of bowl.

Mix in the flour, cocoa powder, and salt, beating just until combined. Then add 2 tbsp. of ice water, beating just until moistened. Do not overmix.

Press dough into a 4" disk. Wrap in plastic wrap and chill for 2 hours or until firm.

Slightly overlap 2 sheets of plastic wrap on a damp surface. Unwrap and place chilled Vanilla Dough on plastic wrap. Cover dough with 2 additional sheets of overlapping plastic wrap. Roll dough, still covered, into a 12x8" rectangle. Place dough in freezer for 5 minutes or until plastic wrap can easily be removed. Remove top sheets of plastic wrap.

Slightly overlap 2 sheets of plastic wrap on a damp surface. Unwrap and place chilled Chocolate Dough on plastic wrap. Cover dough with 2 additional sheets of overlapping plastic wrap. Roll dough, still covered, into a 12x8" rectangle. Place dough in freezer for 5 minutes or until plastic wrap can easily be removed. Remove top sheets of plastic wrap.

Place Vanilla Dough on top of Chocolate Dough, plastic wrap side up. Remove plastic wrap from Vanilla Dough; turn dough over onto a lightly floured surface. Remove plastic wrap from Chocolate Dough.

Cut dough stack in half crosswise to form 2 (6x8") rectangles. Stack 1 rectangle on top of the other, alternating vanilla and chocolate dough. Freeze 10 minutes or until firm.

Cut the dough crosswise into 6 (6x1x⅓") strips. Stack 2 strips on top of each other to form a stack, alternating vanilla and chocolate dough to form a striped pattern; wrap in plastic wrap, pressing gently.

Repeat procedure with remaining 4 strips to form 2 stacks (there will be 3 stacks total). Chill 45 minutes or until very firm.

Heat oven to 375 degrees. Line cookie sheets with parchment paper.

Working with one stack at a time, unwrap dough. Quickly and carefully, slice each stack into 12 slices. Place dough slices 2" apart on prepared sheets.

Bake for 11 to 12 minutes. Cool 5 minutes, then remove from cookie sheets to wire racks to cool completely. Makes about 3 dozen.

Whoa, baby. Who knew even a zebra could be envious of another's stripes?

You'll "wow" them with this one, and you'll love how easy these Chocolate-Topped Marshmallow Bars are to make.

Chocolate-Topped Marshmallow Bars

This marshmallow filling is deceptively easy to make, and this bar is like eating an adult version of a marshmallow peep with a crust!

1½ cups unbleached, all-purpose flour
¾ cup confectioners' sugar, sifted
¾ cup unsalted butter, cold and cut
   into pieces

MARSHMALLOW FILLING

1 cup water, divided
2 tbsp. unflavored gelatin
2 cups granulated sugar
1 tsp. pure lemon extract
¼ tsp. lemon juice
1 tbsp. fresh lemon zest, finely grated

CHOCOLATE TOPPING

16 oz. milk chocolate, coarsely chopped
2 tbsp. shortening
1 tbsp. unsalted butter

BEV'S BITES

Sticky, gooey, and yummy—a thin, non-stick spatula works best for bar removal.

Heat oven to 350 degrees.

Using an electric mixer, beat together the flour, confectioners' sugar, and butter until crumbly. Press mixture onto bottom of an ungreased 13x9" baking pan.

Bake for 12 to 14 minutes or just until crust is a light golden color. Cool completely on a wire rack.

For the Marshmallow Filling: In a large bowl, combine ½ cup of water and 2 tbsp. gelatin; set aside. In a medium saucepan, combine the granulated sugar and ½ cup of water; bring to a boil. Boil for 2 minutes. Pour sugar/water syrup over gelatin; mix well. Cool 5 minutes in the refrigerator.

Using an electric mixer, beat gelatin mixture for 6 to 12 minutes at highest speed until very thick. Mixture will go from clear to milky and look like marshmallow fluff. Add lemon extract and lemon juice and beat to combine. Fold in lemon zest. Spoon and spread over cooled crust. Refrigerate about 2 hours or until set.

For the Chocolate Topping: In a small saucepan, over very low heat, melt the milk chocolate with the shortening and butter, stirring until mixture is smooth. Spread or drizzle over filling.

Cut into bars before topping sets. Cool completely. Makes about 2 dozen.

Chocolate Chip Cookie Brownie Bars

This is what happens when two favorites collide—spoonfuls of chocolate chip cookie dough atop a fudgy brownie layer! A favorite from my cookbook, BROWNIES to Die For!

BROWNIE BASE

4 oz. unsweetened chocolate, coarsely chopped
⅔ cup unsalted butter
2 cups granulated sugar
4 large eggs, lightly beaten
1 tsp. pure vanilla extract
1¼ cups unbleached, all-purpose flour
1 tsp. baking powder
1 tsp. salt

CHOCOLATE CHIP COOKIE DOUGH TOPPING

¾ cup unsalted butter, melted
¾ cup firmly packed light brown sugar
½ cup granulated sugar
2 large eggs, lightly beaten
1 tsp. pure vanilla extract
1¾ cups unbleached, all-purpose flour
¾ tsp. baking soda
½ tsp. salt
1½ cups mini semisweet chocolate chips

Heat oven to 350 degrees. Lightly grease a 13x9" baking pan. Line pan with foil, then lightly (and gently so as not to tear it) grease foil.

For the Brownie Base: Melt the chocolate and butter in a medium saucepan, over low heat, stirring to blend. Remove pan from heat and whisk in sugar, eggs, and vanilla.

Stir in flour, baking powder, and salt. Spread into prepared pan.

For the Chocolate Chip Cookie Dough Topping: Using an electric mixer, in a large bowl, beat the butter and sugars until light and fluffy. Add eggs and vanilla and beat until creamy. Scrape down sides and bottom of bowl.

Mix in the flour, baking soda, and salt. Stir in chocolate chips. Top Brownie Base with spoonfuls of Cookie Dough Topping, distributing as evenly as possible.

Bake for 55 to 65 minutes or until a cake tester or toothpick inserted in the center comes out with a few moist crumbs attached. Cool completely on a wire rack.

When completely cool, invert onto a large cutting board and gently remove foil. Reflip onto another large cutting board so the Chocolate Chip Cookie Topping is right side up. Cut into bars. Makes about 3 dozen.

White Chocolate Aloha Bars

A surprisingly chewy confection, even better if allowed to sit overnight so the flavors can meld.

6 oz. white chocolate, coarsely chopped
5 tbsp. unsalted butter, room temperature
2 large eggs
1 cup granulated sugar
1 tsp. pure vanilla extract
1 cup unbleached, all-purpose flour
½ tsp. baking powder
¼ tsp. salt
½ cup roasted macadamia nuts, coarsely chopped
2 oz. bittersweet chocolate, finely chopped

Heat oven to 350 degrees. Lightly grease and flour a 9" square baking pan. Tap out any excess flour.

In a medium saucepan, over very low heat, melt the white chocolate and butter, stirring constantly, until smooth. Remove saucepan from heat and cool to room temperature.

Using an electric mixer, in a large bowl, beat together the eggs, sugar, and vanilla until mixture is thickened. Beat in white chocolate mixture.

Mix in the flour, baking powder, and salt until well combined. Stir in the nuts and chocolate pieces. Gently spread batter into prepared pan.

Bake in middle of oven for 25 to 32 minutes or until a tester inserted near the center comes out with a few moist crumbs attached.

Cool completely on a wire rack. Cut into bars or squares. Makes about 1 dozen.

Creamy Cheesecake Bars

What a combination of flavors and textures! Using the best quality white chocolate (and, of course, other ingredients) will yield a sinfully divine, blissful no-bake bar.

Unsalted butter, melted, for brushing foil

7½ oz. white chocolate, coarsely chopped

11 oz. chocolate sandwich cookies, about 27 cookies

½ cup heavy (whipping) cream

8 oz. cream cheese, room temperature

3 tbsp. superfine sugar

3 tbsp. fresh lime juice

1 tbsp. fresh lime zest, finely grated

BEV'S BITES

Superfine sugar or caster sugar is more finely granulated and dissolves almost instantly. Granulated sugar may be substituted in this recipe if superfine is not in your pantry.

Line an 8" square baking pan with foil, extending the foil slightly above all sides. Gently brush foil with melted butter.

In a double boiler set over lightly simmering water, melt the white chocolate until smooth. Remove from heat and allow white chocolate to cool slightly.

In a food processor, finely grind the sandwich cookies (perhaps taking a few of the extras to enjoy while these bars are baking!). Add 2 tbsp. of the melted white chocolate and blend until mixture clumps.

Spoon cookie/white chocolate mixture into prepared pan and press onto bottom. Chill while making filling.

Using an electric mixer, beat heavy cream in a medium bowl until soft peaks form; set aside.

In another medium bowl, beat the cream cheese, sugar, lime juice, and zest until smooth. Beat in the remaining white chocolate. Scrape down sides and bottom of bowl.

Fold in whipped cream in 2 additions, then gently spread over prepared crust. Chill until filling is firm and set, at least 3 hours.

Lift cheesecake out of pan using the foil as an aid. Cut into bars and serve, being careful to remove any foil that sticks to bottom. Makes about 12.

Cranberry White Chocolate Blondies

Flavor-wise, there IS a little bit of blondie in all of us.

½ cup unsalted butter, room temperature, plus additional, melted, for brushing foil
½ cup granulated sugar
½ cup firmly packed light brown sugar
¾ tsp. baking powder
¼ tsp. baking soda
¼ tsp. salt
2 large eggs
1 tsp. pure vanilla extract
1 cup unbleached, all-purpose flour, divided
½ cup plus 1 tbsp. dried cranberries, snipped into pieces
½ cup coarsely chopped white chocolate
1 cup fresh cranberries, coarsely chopped

BEV'S BITES

Be sure your white chocolate has cocoa butter listed in the ingredients . . . otherwise, it's simply an overly sweet confectionary coating.

Heat oven to 350 degrees. Line a 9" square baking pan with foil, then lightly brush foil with melted butter.

Using an electric mixer, in a large bowl, beat the butter and sugars until light and fluffy. Scrape down sides and bottom of bowl.

Mix in the baking powder, baking soda, and salt. Beat in the eggs and vanilla until well combined. Scrape down sides and bottom of bowl.

In a small bowl, toss 1 tbsp. of the flour with the dried cranberries and white chocolate pieces just until lightly coated.

Stir the remaining flour into the batter mixture just until blended. Stir in the cranberries and white chocolate pieces. Gently spread batter into prepared pan and top with the chopped fresh cranberries.

Bake for 22 to 30 minutes or until a toothpick inserted near the center comes out clean. Cool completely on a wire rack.

Use foil overhang as handles and lift the Blondie with the foil from the pan. Cut into bars. Remove foil and serve. Makes about 12.

Shortbread Topped with Chunks of Cranberry Cheesecake Bars

Two totally different textures . . . perfectly tart with a refreshing orange taste.

1 cup unbleached, all-purpose flour
1/4 cup confectioners' sugar, sifted
1/2 cup unsalted butter, cold, cut into pieces

TOPPING

10 oz. cream cheese, room temperature
2 tbsp. granulated sugar
2 tbsp. sour cream
2 large eggs
1 tsp. vanilla
5 tbsp. marmalade, orange or lemon
3/4 cup fresh or frozen (unthawed) cranberries, chopped
2 tbsp. fresh orange zest, finely grated

Heat oven to 350 degrees. Lightly grease a 9" square baking pan.

Place the flour and confectioners' sugar in a food processor, pulsing to combine. Add the butter pieces and pulse just until the dough comes together.

Press the dough gently over the bottom of the prepared pan and about 1" up the sides.

Bake the crust until golden, about 20 minutes. Cool completely on a wire rack.

For the Topping: Using an electric mixer, in a large bowl, beat the cream cheese and granulated sugar together until light and fluffy. Scrape down sides and bottom of bowl.

Add the sour cream and beat the mixture until smooth. Scrape down sides and bottom of bowl.

Add the eggs and vanilla and beat until smooth and creamy. Add the marmalade and beat until blended. Gently mix in the cranberries and zest.

Spoon the cream cheese mixture over the cooled base, smoothing lightly with a thin spatula to distribute evenly.

Bake until the top is light golden around the edges and a tester inserted in the center comes out clean, 35 to 38 minutes.

Cool completely on a wire rack. Cut into squares. Makes about 16.

Raspberry Citrus Bars

Fresh raspberries provide a colorful, refreshing change of pace in this buttery light bar.

1 cup unsalted butter, room temperature
¾ cup confectioners' sugar, sifted plus additional for dusting
2¼ cups unbleached, all-purpose flour, divided
4 large eggs
1½ cups granulated sugar
⅓ cup fresh lemon juice
2 tbsp. fresh orange zest, finely grated
1 tsp. baking powder
1½ cups fresh red raspberries

BEV'S BITES

These bars freeze well. Place in an airtight container and freeze for up to 2 months. Thaw, covered, in the refrigerator.

Heat oven to 350 degrees. Grease a 13x9" baking pan.

Using an electric mixer, in a large bowl, beat together the butter and confectioners' sugar until light and fluffy. Scrape down sides and bottom of bowl.

Mix in 2 cups of the flour, beating until combined. Press crumb mixture onto bottom of prepared pan. Bake for 20 minutes or just until golden.

Using an electric mixer, in a large bowl, combine the eggs, granulated sugar, lemon juice, zest, remaining ¼ cup of the flour, and baking powder. Beat until well combined.

Sprinkle raspberries over crust. Gently pour filling over berries, arranging evenly with a spoon.

Bake for 28 to 32 minutes or until light brown and filling is set. Cool completely on a wire rack.

Cut into bars. Just before serving, sprinkle with confectioners' sugar. Makes about 2½ dozen.

Mostly Crumb (Yum!) Bars with Raspberry Filling

A nutty, crunchy crumb topping sprinkled over a red raspberry filling bursting with flavor.

2¼ cups unbleached, all-purpose flour
1 cup granulated sugar
1 cup coarsely chopped pecans, toasted
1 cup unsalted butter, cold, cut into
  pieces
1 large egg
10 oz. jar red raspberry fruit spread or
  preserves

BEV'S BITES

Having something this good easily at hand is every hostess's dream. Cover and freeze these Mostly Crumb (Yum!) Bars for up to 1 month.

Heat oven to 350 degrees. Lightly grease an 8" square baking pan.

Using an electric mixer, in a large mixing bowl, beat together the flour, sugar, pecans, butter, and egg just until mixture is crumbly.

Reserve 1½ cups of the crumb mix; set aside.

Press the remaining crumb mix onto the bottom of the prepared pan. Spread the fruit spread or preserves to within ¼" of the edge.

Using lightly floured hands, top with reserved crumb mix, sprinkling as evenly as possible.

Bake for 40 to 48 minutes or until a light golden brown.

Cool completely on a wire rack. Cut into bars. Makes about 16.

My love of crumb cakes and fresh fruit flavors prompted my creation of these sinful Mostly Crumb (Yum!) Bars with Raspberry Filling.

Bev's Bodacious Blueberry Bars

Courageously loaded with blueberry flavor, these bars will give you your antioxidant fix.

1½ cups quick-cooking oats
1 cup unbleached, all-purpose flour
¾ cup firmly packed light brown sugar
¾ cup unsalted butter, cold, cut into pieces
1 cup fresh or frozen (unthawed) blueberries
⅛ cup dried blueberries
¾ cup blueberry fruit spread or jam
1½ tsp. fresh lemon zest, finely grated

Heat oven to 350 degrees. Line an 8" square baking pan with foil and set aside.

In a medium mixing bowl, combine the oats, flour, and brown sugar, blending well. Cut in the butter until mixture resembles coarse crumbs. Reserve 1 cup of the crumb mix.

Press remaining oat mix onto bottom of prepared pan. Bake for 22 to 25 minutes or just until crust turns a light golden brown.

In a medium mixing bowl, combine the blueberries, fruit spread, and zest. Gently spread over baked crust. Sprinkle with reserved oat mix, pressing lightly into blueberry mixture.

Bake for 25 to 30 more minutes or just until the crumb top is a light golden color. Cool completely on a wire rack.

Cut into bars. Makes about 2 dozen.

Apricot Showpiece Linzer Bars

Along with a kiss of lemon, this cookie is an apricot lover's dream with plenty of apricot and a delightful tang without being over-loaded or messy. A bar you'll make again and again.

2 cups plus 3 tbsp. unbleached, all-purpose flour
$1/2$ cup granulated sugar
$1/4$ tsp. salt
$2\frac{1}{2}$ tsp. fresh lemon zest, finely grated
15 tbsp. unsalted butter, cold, cut into pieces
2 large egg yolks, lightly beaten

FILLING

8 oz. dried apricots, finely chopped
$3/4$ cup apricot preserves or fruit spread
2 tbsp. fresh lemon juice
1 large egg, lightly beaten

BEV'S BITES

Don't let the lattice top intimidate you. I've taught this technique in hands-on classes and used it many times. It's a very easy process and the end result is something to be proud of.

Heat oven to 375 degrees. Line a 9" square baking pan with foil, being sure that foil hangs over the edges of the pan. Lightly grease the foil with melted butter.

Pulse the flour, sugar, salt, and lemon zest in a food processor until blended. Add the butter and pulse just until the mixture resembles coarse crumbs.

With the machine running, pour the blended yolks in a steady stream through the feed tube and process just until the dough comes together.

Divide the dough into two thirds and one third portions. Gently press the larger portion evenly in the bottom of the prepared pan, taking it about $1/2$" up the sides.

Bake 30 minutes or just until crust is a light golden color.

While the crust is baking, prepare the lattice top. Roll out the remaining dough between pieces of waxed paper or parchment paper to form a $9\frac{1}{2}$" square. Place this, still on the paper, on a tray or plate in the freezer while preparing the filling.

For the Filling: In a small saucepan, combine the apricots with enough water to cover. Bring to a boil over medium heat. Boil until soft, then drain the apricots, patting them dry with paper towels.

In a small bowl, combine the plumped apricot pieces with the preserves and lemon juice, mixing well.

Spread the apricot filling over the baked base. Raise the oven temperature to 400 degrees.

Remove the dough from the freezer and peel off the top piece of paper. Cut the dough into 14 strips approximately $1/2$" wide. Carefully place half of the strips across the filling, about 1" apart. The first and last strip should be touching the sides of the pan.

Repeat with the remaining strips, placing them perpendicular to the first set of strips, in a lattice pattern.

Press the ends into the dough. Brush the beaten egg over the lattice strips.

Bake until lattice is golden, about 40 to 45 minutes. Cool for 30 minutes on a wire rack.

Lift the baked mixture out of the pan using the foil overhang handles to assist. Cool completely on a wire rack. Makes 16 bars, but could be cut smaller to make 25 bars.

Showpiece? These Apricot Showpiece Linzer Bars will never last long!

Crumb-Topped Pineapple Bars

A taste of the tropics baked into a buttery, refreshing fruit bar that's so easy to make.

1½ cups unbleached, all-purpose flour
¾ cup unsalted butter, room temperature
1 cup granulated sugar, divided
¼ cup cornstarch
20 oz. can crushed pineapple, well drained
2 tsp. fresh lemon juice
⅓ cup sliced almonds or chopped macadamia nuts, toasted

Heat oven to 350 degrees. Lightly grease a 13x9" baking pan.

Using an electric mixer, in a large bowl, beat together the flour, butter, and ½ cup of the granulated sugar until mixture is crumbly. Scrape down sides and bottom of bowl.

Measure and set aside 1 cup of the crumb mix.

Press remaining crumb mix onto bottom of the prepared pan. Bake for 10 minutes.

While crust is baking, stir together the remaining ½ cup of sugar and cornstarch in a medium saucepan. Add the well-drained pineapple and lemon juice; mix well to combine.

Cook over medium heat, stirring constantly, until mixture becomes very thick.

Spoon filling over hot crust. With lightly floured hands, sprinkle reserved crumb mixture as evenly as possible over filling. Top with toasted almonds or macadamia nuts.

Return to oven and bake for 16 to 20 minutes or until a light golden brown.

Cool completely on a wire rack. Cut into bars. Makes about 3 dozen.

Coconut-Topped Pineapple Cheesecake Bars

Elegant enough for a dinner party dessert and just perfect for every-day dinners.

1 cup unbleached, all-purpose flour
½ cup granulated sugar
½ cup unsalted butter, room temperature

FILLING

2 tbsp. granulated sugar
8 oz. cream cheese, room temperature
2 tbsp. milk, whole or 2 percent
1 tsp. pure vanilla extract
1 large egg
20 oz. can crushed pineapple, well drained

TOPPING

1¼ cups unsweetened coconut
1 tbsp. unsalted butter, melted and cooled

Heat oven to 350 degrees.

In a small bowl, stir together the flour, sugar, and butter until mixture forms coarse crumbs. Press onto bottom of an ungreased 13x9" baking pan.

Bake for 10 to 14 minutes or just until lightly browned.

For the Filling: Using an electric mixer, in a medium bowl, beat together the sugar, cream cheese, milk, vanilla, and egg until smooth. Scrape down sides and bottom of bowl.

Stir in the well-drained pineapple. Gently spoon over partially baked crust.

For the Topping: In a small bowl, stir together the coconut and butter. Sprinkle over Filling.

Return pan to oven and bake for 16 to 20 more minutes or until filling is set and coconut is a light golden brown. Cool completely on a wire rack.

Cut into bars. Makes about 3 dozen.

Almost Like Key Lime Bars

Forget the pie crust; this simple bar cookie will satisfy your key lime cravings without all the extra work.

1 cup fresh lime juice
2 14 oz. cans sweetened condensed milk
1 tsp. fresh lime zest, finely grated
1½ cups unbleached, all-purpose flour
½ cup granulated sugar
½ cup very finely chopped roasted macadamia nuts
½ cup unsalted butter, cold and cut into pieces
½ cup plus 3 tbsp. flaked coconut

Heat oven to 350 degrees. In a large bowl, whisk together the lime juice, condensed milk, and zest. Cover loosely with plastic wrap and set aside; mixture will thicken slightly.

In a large bowl, combine the flour, sugar, and macadamia nuts. Cut in the butter until mixture resembles coarse crumbs.

Pat crumb mix evenly onto bottom of 13x9" baking pan. Bake for 15 to 17 minutes or just until edges begin to turn a light golden brown.

Pour lime juice mixture over hot crust. Sprinkle with coconut and continue to bake for 15 to 18 minutes or just until filling is set.

Cool completely on a wire rack. Cut into bars and serve. Makes about 3½ dozen.

*These Lemon Bars and Lime Bars don't need to fight it out
for a spot on your dessert buffet; there will be
lots of room (and requests) for both.*

Lemon Bars and Lime Bars

These are the most refreshing bars I know—light and flavorful and bursting with bright flavors.

LEMON BARS

2 cups plus ¼ cup unbleached, all-purpose flour, divided
½ cup confectioners' sugar, sifted plus extra for dusting
1 cup unsalted butter, room temperature
4 large eggs
2 cups granulated sugar
1 tsp. baking powder
½ cup plus 1 tbsp. fresh lemon juice
2 tbsp. fresh lemon zest, finely grated

BEV'S BITES ———————

Make these bars extra special: Serve the lemon bars with fresh red raspberries and the lime bars with slices of kiwi.

Heat oven to 350 degrees.

Using an electric mixer, in a large bowl, blend 2 cups of the flour with the confectioners' sugar and butter until mixture is crumbly.

Press the mixture, with lightly floured hands, evenly onto the bottom of an ungreased 13x9" baking pan. Bake for 18 to 22 minutes or just until crust is a light golden in color.

While crust is baking, make the filling. In a large bowl, whisk together the eggs and granulated sugar. Add in the remaining ¼ cup of flour, baking powder, lemon juice, and zest.

Remove the pan from the oven and quickly pour the lemon filling mixture over the warm crust. Return to oven and bake for 22 to 25 minutes or until the filling is a light golden color.

Cool completely on a wire rack.

When ready to serve, cut into bars and sprinkle each with additional sifted confectioners' sugar. Makes about 2 dozen.

LIME BARS

Substitute ½ cup plus 1 tbsp. fresh lime juice for lemon juice. Substitute 1 tbsp. fresh lime zest, finely grated for lemon zest.

Zucchini Lemon Bars

A flavorful cakelike bar, just as easily at home for breakfast as for an afternoon snack.

2 cups unbleached, all-purpose flour
1 cup granulated sugar
1 tsp. baking soda
¼ tsp. salt
½ cup nonfat lemon or plain yogurt
¼ cup unsalted butter, melted
1 tbsp. fresh lemon zest, finely grated
2 tbsp. fresh lemon juice
1 cup shredded zucchini
4 tbsp. confectioners' sugar, sifted

BEV'S BITES

Don't let the dryness of the batter fool you; it will yield a tasty, moist bar.

Heat oven to 350 degrees. Lightly grease a 9" square baking pan.

In a large bowl, combine the flour, sugar, baking soda, and salt, mixing until blended.

In a small bowl, whisk together the yogurt, butter, zest, and juice. Add the yogurt mixture to the flour mixture, stirring just until moistened. Blend in zucchini. Do not overmix.

Spread into prepared pan. Bake for 30 minutes or until a toothpick inserted in center comes out clean.

Cool completely on a wire rack. Sprinkle with confectioners' sugar, then cut into bars. Makes 12.

*Sneak some zucchini on my neighbor's porch? Not when I can turn
that summer squash into these tasty Zucchini Lemon Bars.*

Pumpkin Crumb Bars

The all-time favorite flavor of pumpkin pie mixed and baked in an easy, breezy pumpkin crumb bar.

1⅓ cups unbleached, all-purpose flour
½ cup firmly packed light brown sugar
¾ cup granulated sugar, divided
¾ cup unsalted butter, cold, plus
    additional, melted, for brushing foil
1 cup old-fashioned rolled oats (not
    quick cooking)
½ cup chopped pecans, toasted
8 oz. cream cheese, room temperature
3 large eggs
15 oz. can pumpkin purée
1 tbsp. pumpkin pie spice

BEV'S BITES ————————

To cut cold butter into a dry mixture, use a pastry blender, 2 knives, or 2 forks. Work quickly so butter remains cold.

DON'T use pumpkin pie filling, as it contains spices and other ingredients.

Heat oven to 350 degrees. Line a 13x9" baking pan with foil, extending ends of foil at least 1" over sides of pan. Lightly brush foil with melted butter.

Mix the flour, brown sugar, and ¼ cup of the granulated sugar in a medium bowl, then cut in the butter until mixture resembles coarse crumbs. Stir in oats and pecans.

Reserve 1 cup of the crumb mixture, then press remaining mixture onto bottom of prepared pan.

Bake for 15 minutes or until light golden around edges.

While mixture is baking, using an electric mixer, in a large bowl, beat together the cream cheese, remaining ½ cup of granulated sugar, eggs, pumpkin, and pumpkin pie spice until well blended. Gently pour over warm crust. With lightly floured hands, sprinkle with reserved crumb mixture, distributing as evenly as possible.

Bake for 25 to 30 minutes until filling looks set and topping is a golden brown. Cool completely on a wire rack.

Use foil overhang as handles and gently lift baked mixture with foil from pan. Cut into bars. Makes about 24.

Sweet Potato Orange Bars

Sweet potatoes, cooked and mashed, are a welcome addition to this moist, flavorful frosted bar cookie.

4 large eggs
1³⁄₄ cups mashed, cooked sweet potatoes
1²⁄₃ cups granulated sugar
1 cup light olive oil or canola oil
2 cups unbleached, all-purpose flour
2 tsp. baking powder
2 tsp. ground cinnamon
2 tsp. fresh orange zest, finely grated
1 tsp. baking soda
¹⁄₂ tsp. freshly grated nutmeg
¹⁄₄ tsp. salt
¹⁄₂ cup coarsely chopped pecans, toasted
¹⁄₂ cup seedless raisins

FROSTING

6 oz. cream cheese, room temperature
¹⁄₂ cup unsalted butter, room temperature
2 tsp. pure vanilla extract
4 cups confectioners' sugar, sifted

Heat oven to 350 degrees.

Using an electric mixer, in a large bowl, beat together the eggs, sweet potato, granulated sugar, and oil until well blended. Scrape down sides and bottom of bowl.

Add flour, baking powder, cinnamon, zest, baking soda, nutmeg, and salt. Mix until blended. Scrape down sides and bottom of bowl.

Stir in pecans and raisins. Spread batter into an ungreased 15x10" jellyroll pan. Bake for 22 to 28 minutes or until a toothpick inserted in the center comes out clean.

Cool completely on a wire rack.

For the Frosting: Using an electric mixer, in a large bowl, beat together the cream cheese, butter, and vanilla until light and fluffy. Gradually add in the confectioners' sugar, beating until smooth.

Frost with Cream Cheese Frosting. Cut into bars. Makes about 2 dozen.

*I'm not entirely convinced that one piece of this
Browned-Butter Banana Bar will be enough.*

Browned-Butter Banana Bars

A moist, rich banana bar enhanced with the sophisticated flavors of a browned-butter frosting.

1 cup granulated sugar
1/2 cup firmly packed light brown sugar
1/2 cup unsalted butter, room temperature
2 cups (3 or 4 large) mashed, ripe
   bananas
8 oz. sour cream
2 large eggs
2 tsp. pure vanilla extract
2 cups unbleached, all-purpose flour
2 tsp. ground cinnamon
1 tsp. salt
1 tsp. baking soda
1/2 cup coarsely chopped walnuts, toasted

BROWNED-BUTTER FROSTING

1/4 cup unsalted butter, room temperature
2 cups confectioners' sugar, sifted
3 tbsp. milk, whole or 2 percent

Heat oven to 375 degrees. Lightly grease a 15x10" jellyroll pan.

Using an electric mixer, in a large bowl, cream together the sugars and butter until light and fluffy. Scrape down sides and bottom of bowl.

Beat in the bananas, sour cream, eggs, and vanilla.

Blend in the flour, cinnamon, salt, and baking soda just until blended. Scrape down sides and bottom of bowl.

Stir in the walnuts, then pour batter into prepared pan. Bake for 20 minutes or until toothpick inserted in the center comes out clean.

Cool completely on a wire rack.

For the Browned-Butter Frosting: In a small saucepan, cook butter over low heat until lightly browned and bubbly. This only takes a few minutes, so watch carefully so that the butter doesn't burn.

Whisk in the confectioners' sugar and milk; beat until creamy. Working quickly, as the frosting hardens fast, spread evenly over top. When Frosting sets, cut into bars. Makes about 18.

Swirled Gingerbread Cream Cheese Bars

An easy to make (and enjoy) gingerbread bar cookie swirled with cream cheese and topped with an equally easy sweet cream cheese frosting.

1¼ cups unbleached, all-purpose flour
2½ tsp. ground ginger
1½ tsp. ground cinnamon
¼ tsp. baking soda
¼ tsp. salt
¾ cup unsalted butter, room temperature, plus additional, melted, for brushing foil
1¼ cups granulated sugar, divided
1 large egg
⅓ cup molasses
8 oz. cream cheese, room temperature
2 tsp. pure vanilla extract

Heat oven to 350 degrees. Line a 13x9" baking pan with foil. Lightly brush foil with melted butter.

In a small bowl, mix together the flour, ginger, cinnamon, baking soda, and salt.

Using an electric mixer, in a large bowl, beat the butter with ¾ cup of the granulated sugar until light and fluffy. Scrape down sides and bottom of bowl.

Beat in egg until well blended. Mix in flour mixture until combined. Scrape down sides and bottom of bowl.

Stir in molasses and 3 tbsp. water just until blended. Do not overmix.

Gently spread into prepared pan.

Using an electric mixer, in a medium bowl, beat cream cheese until smooth. Beat in remaining ½ cup of the granulated sugar and the vanilla. Scrape down sides and bottom of bowl.

Reserve ½ cup of the frosting; cover and refrigerate remaining frosting until ready to use. Spoon teaspoonful dollops of the reserved ½ cup of frosting over the gingerbread batter in pan. With a knife or spatula, ever so gently swirl frosting throughout the batter to marbleize.

Bake for 28 to 35 minutes or until a toothpick inserted in center comes out clean. Cool in pan on a wire rack for 15 minutes. Carefully lift out of pan using foil. Cool completely on a wire rack.

Invert and gently peel off foil. Invert again so bottom is down, then spread refrigerated frosting over gingerbread. Cut into bars. Makes about 2 dozen.

Gingerbread Streusel Thins

These squares and a dollop of freshly whipped cream go hand-in-hand.

¼ cup unsalted butter, room temperature
½ cup granulated sugar
1 cup unbleached, all-purpose flour
1 tsp. ground ginger
1½ tsp. ground cinnamon
½ tsp. ground allspice
⅛ tsp. salt
½ tsp. baking soda
½ cup buttermilk
¼ cup molasses
1 large egg
1 cup heavy (whipping) cream

BEV'S BITES

Make your whipped-cream topping extra special: Combine ¼ tsp. granulated sugar with 1 tsp. ground cinnamon and add to the cream before whipping.

Heat oven to 350 degrees. Grease the bottom only of a 13x9" baking pan.

Using an electric mixer, in a large bowl, beat together the butter and sugar until light and fluffy. Scrape down sides and bottom of bowl.

Stir in the flour, ginger, cinnamon, allspice, and salt, mixing just until crumbly. Set aside ⅓ cup of the crumb mixture for the topping.

To remaining crumb mixture, add baking soda, stirring to blend. Mix in buttermilk, molasses, and egg; blend well.

Pour batter into greased pan. With clean, dry fingers, sprinkle with reserved crumb mixture.

Bake for 8 to 11 minutes or until a toothpick inserted in center comes out clean. This is a thin batter, so be careful not to overbake.

Cool completely on a wire rack. Cut into bars. Makes about 16.

Gingerbread Bars with a Touch of Whole Wheat

I love the nutty flavor whole-wheat flour gives to these moist, flavorful bars.

½ cup unsalted butter, room temperature
1 cup unbleached, all-purpose flour
½ cup whole-wheat flour
½ cup molasses
½ cup hot water
¼ cup firmly packed light brown sugar
1 large egg
¾ tsp. baking powder
¾ tsp. ground cinnamon
½ tsp. ground ginger
¼ tsp. baking soda
¼ tsp. salt

FROSTING

⅓ cup unsalted butter, room temperature
4 cups confectioners' sugar, sifted
¼ cup pure maple syrup
½ tsp. pure vanilla extract

BEV'S BITES

I prefer a light-flavored Barbados molasses to the more assertive Blackstrap molasses in this recipe.

Heat oven to 375 degrees. Lightly grease a 13x9" baking pan.

Using an electric mixer, in a large bowl, beat the butter until light and fluffy. Scrape down sides and bottom of bowl.

Mix in the flours, molasses, ½ cup of hot water, brown sugar, egg, baking powder, cinnamon, ginger, baking soda, and salt. Beat until well combined. Scrape down sides and bottom of bowl.

Spread batter into prepared pan. Bake for 20 to 25 minutes or until a toothpick inserted in the center comes out with a moist crumb or two attached.

Cool completely on a wire rack.

For the Frosting: Using an electric mixer, in a large bowl, beat together the butter, confectioners' sugar, maple syrup, and vanilla until smooth. Stir in an additional tsp. or two of water if needed to reach desired spreading consistency.

Spread over cooled bars. Cut into bars. Makes about 2½ dozen.

Pine Nut Bars

This delightful, change-of-pace bar is perfect after a Mediterranean feast or would go well cut into very small pieces on an appetizer table.

1 cup plus 1 tbsp. unbleached, all-purpose flour, divided
1 cup quick-cooking oats
1/2 cup confectioners' sugar, sifted
1/2 tsp. baking powder
1/2 cup plus 1/3 cup unsalted butter, room temperature, divided
1/3 cup heavy (whipping) cream
1 tbsp. milk, whole or 2 percent
1/2 cup granulated sugar
1 1/4 cups pine nuts, lightly toasted

BEV'S BITES ——————

Pine nuts have a mild flavor and are traditionally used in pesto recipes. They turn rancid quickly so store them in the refrigerator or the freezer and toast lightly before using.

I prefer to toast nuts in a dry skillet atop the stove, removing from the heat when they are fragrant. There is often a fine line between turning golden and burning, especially when left unattended to bake in the oven.

One final note, these bars have the best flavor if allowed to sit for a day before indulging.

Heat oven to 350 degrees. Lightly grease a 13x9" pan.

In a large bowl, combine 1 cup of the flour, oats, confectioners' sugar, and baking powder.

Cut in 1/2 cup of the butter until crumbly and mixture resembles coarse crumbs. Press in bottom of prepared pan and bake for 12 to 14 minutes or until crust is set.

While crust is baking, in a small saucepan over medium-low heat, combine the cream, milk, and the remaining 1/3 cup of butter, stirring until blended and butter begins to melt. Stir in the sugar and remaining 1 tbsp. of the flour. Bring to a boil and boil for 3 minutes, stirring.

Pour mixture over warm crust; sprinkle with toasted pine nuts. Return to the oven and bake for an additional 6 to 8 minutes or until topping bubbles.

Cool completely on a wire rack. Cut into bars. Makes about 2 1/2 dozen.

NOLA Cheesecake Squares

New Orleans praline flavors are prominent in this elegant yet casual bar cookie.

2½ cups unbleached, all-purpose flour
1 cup unsalted butter, melted and cooled
⅔ cup finely chopped pecans, toasted
2 tbsp. confectioners' sugar, sifted

FILLING

24 oz. cream cheese, room temperature
4 large eggs
14 oz. can sweetened condensed milk
⅔ cup granulated sugar
1 tbsp. pure vanilla extract

TOPPING

1 cup firmly packed light brown sugar
¼ cup firmly packed dark brown sugar
1 cup heavy (whipping) cream
1 cup finely chopped pecans, toasted
1½ tsp. pure vanilla extract

BEV'S BITES

Foil line your baking pan and lightly brush with melted butter for even easier removal of the squares from the pan.

Heat oven to 350 degrees.

In a large bowl, combine the flour, melted butter, pecans, and the confectioners' sugar until well mixed. Press crumb mix onto the bottom of an ungreased 13x9" baking pan.

Bake for 15 to 18 minutes or just until crust is a light golden brown around the edges.

For the Filling: Using an electric mixer, in a large bowl, beat the cream cheese until smooth. Scrape down sides and bottom of bowl.

Beat in eggs until combined. Stir in sweetened condensed milk, sugar, and vanilla. Scrape down sides and bottom of bowl. Pour Filling over baked crust.

Bake for 35 to 40 minutes or until mixture is set. Cool completely on a wire rack.

For the Topping: In a medium saucepan, combine the light and dark brown sugars and heavy cream. Cook, stirring over medium heat, until mixture boils. Reduce heat to low and simmer for 10 minutes.

Remove saucepan from heat. Stir in the chopped pecans and vanilla. Gently spoon topping over cheesecake filling.

Cover loosely and chill for at least 2 hours (up to 24 hours) before serving. Cut into bars, carefully dipping knife into warm water and wiping gently between slices. Makes about 3 dozen.

Spicy Butterscotch Bars

Brown sugar and butter give these bars their oh so butterscotchy profile, and a hint of ground ginger adds the rest.

1½ cups unbleached, all-purpose flour
½ cup unsalted butter, room temperature
¼ cup granulated sugar

FILLING

1½ cups firmly packed light brown
   sugar
¾ cup unbleached, all-purpose flour
⅓ cup unsalted butter, room temperature
2 large eggs
1½ tsp. pure vanilla extract
¾ tsp. baking powder
½ tsp. salt
½ tsp. ground ginger
1½ cups finely chopped pecans, toasted

GLAZE

3 tbsp. unsalted butter, room temperature
¾ cup confectioners' sugar, sifted
1 tsp. brown rice syrup or dark corn
   syrup
1 tsp. pure vanilla extract

Heat oven to 350 degrees.

Using an electric mixer, in a medium bowl, combine the flour, butter, and sugar. Beat at low speed until well mixed. Scrape down sides and bottom of bowl. Mixture will be crumbly.

Press crumb mixture onto bottom of ungreased 13x9" baking pan. Bake for 12 to 15 minutes or just until edges are a light golden brown.

For the Filling: In a large bowl, stir together the brown sugar, flour, butter, eggs, vanilla, baking powder, salt, and ground ginger until well mixed. Stir in the pecans. Gently spoon over hot crust.

Bake for 22 to 30 minutes or until a toothpick inserted in center comes out with a moist crumb or two attached. Cool completely on a wire rack.

For the Glaze: In a small saucepan, melt the butter just until it begins to brown. Watch carefully so butter doesn't burn! Remove from heat and cool for 5 minutes.

Whisk the confectioners' sugar, syrup, and vanilla into the browned butter, adding enough hot water to reach desired glazing consistency. Spread Glaze over cooled bars. Let stand for 15 minutes or more before cutting bars. Makes about 3 dozen.

COOKIES WITH A HERITAGE

I'd trade a bad hair day for a good Hint of Lemon with Pecan Biscotti day anytime!

What is a cookie with a heritage?

Somewhere in your lineage is (or was) a mom, nana, aunt, or great grandmother who baked up a memory, a cookie that was a signature of your (and their) heritage, lovingly passed on from generation to generation.

This chapter offers up an eclectic mix of heritage cookies, a salute to generations of bakers who prepared those tasty morsels for us.

Bake a heritage cookie—pass it on!

Cookie thoughts from John Shaffer

food stylist, food photographer, and original cookie monster!

As Bev and I put together this cookie book, I became aware of how cookies bring back family memories of baking with moms and grandmothers, decorating holiday cookies, the aromas of sugar cookies baking, and eating wedding cake cookies at an aunt's home.

My mom kept the wooden cutting board and red tin scoop I made for her in seventh-grade shop class, displaying those items in her kitchen until she was in her late eighties. We, too, have collected cookie cutters and family kitchen paraphernalia for many years, and I suspect many families do the same in an effort to tie them to their youth.

COOKIES to Die For!, more than any other cookbook, has brought me back to the sweet memories of the past. Scattered throughout this book are props from that past . . . my red tin scoop, Bev's mom's small sieve with its green plastic handle, a large collection of more than one hundred of our eclectic mix of cookie cutters, and more sweet memories in the making.

A Hint of Lemon with Pecan Biscotti

These are meant to be flavorful and crunchy, with a hint of lemon that pulls it all together.

1¼ cups granulated sugar
⅓ cup unsalted butter, room temperature
¼ cup fresh lemon juice
3 large eggs
2 tsp. fresh lemon zest, finely grated
1 tsp. pure vanilla extract
3¼ cups plus 2 tbsp. unbleached, all-purpose flour, divided
¾ cup finely chopped pecans, toasted
1 tsp. baking soda
½ tsp. salt

BEV'S BITES

When making biscotti, be sure to leave plenty of space between the dough rolls so they don't spread and bake together.

After the first bake time, the rolls will be slightly crunchy. Using a serrated knife to slice them works well to help prevent crumbling.

Heat oven to 375 degrees. Line cookie sheets with parchment paper.

Using an electric mixer, in a large bowl, beat together the sugar and butter until light and fluffy. Mix in the lemon juice, eggs, zest, and vanilla, beating until well blended. Scrape down sides and bottom of bowl.

Mix in the 3¼ cups of flour, pecans, baking soda, and salt. Dough will be sticky.

Sprinkle a large piece of foil with the additional flour. Shape dough, with lightly floured hands, into 2 (13") logs on foil. Remove from foil and place on prepared pans, spacing 4" apart. Flatten logs lightly with your hands.

Bake for 22 to 30 minutes or just until a light brown and logs are firm to the touch. Cool on cookie sheets on wire cooling racks for 10 minutes.

Reduce oven temperature to 300 degrees. Carefully place each log, one at a time, on a cutting board and cut into ½" slices. Arrange slices on prepared cookie sheets. Bake for 10 minutes. Turn slices and bake for an additional 5 to 10 minutes or until crisp and a light golden brown. Makes about 3½ dozen.

*Wrap it up and take it to a party, to the office, or
to someone special. These Poppy Seed Lemon Biscotti are always an
appreciated gift from your kitchen.*

Poppy Seed Lemon Biscotti

This is a wonderful dough to work with, so make these often to serve with a cup of your favorite hot beverage or to give as a hostess gift.

1/2 cup granulated sugar
5 tbsp. unsalted butter, room temperature
2 tsp. fresh lemon zest, finely grated
2 large eggs
1 tsp. pure vanilla extract
2 tbsp. poppy seeds
2 cups unbleached, all-purpose flour
2 tsp. baking powder

ICING

1 1/2 cups confectioners' sugar, sifted
1/2 tsp. fresh lemon zest, finely grated
5 tsp. fresh lemon juice or more as needed

Heat oven to 375 degrees. Line cookie sheets with parchment paper.

Using an electric mixer, in a large bowl, beat the sugar, butter, and 2 tsp. of the lemon zest until light and fluffy. Scrape down sides and bottom of bowl.

Add eggs, beating well to combine. Stir in the vanilla then poppy seeds.

Mix in the flour and baking powder, stirring until blended.

Divide the dough in half. Working on a parchment-paper-lined baking sheet with floured hands, form each piece of dough into a flattish log 12" long by 1 1/2" wide.

Arrange the logs at least 3" apart on another parchment-paper-lined cookie sheet. Flatten logs to make them no more than 1" thick. Bake for 15 to 18 minutes or until loaves feel firm to the touch and let them cool on the baking sheet on a wire rack for 10 minutes.

Reduce oven temperature to 350 degrees.

Carefully remove the logs, one at a time, to a large cutting board. Cut the logs (with a serrated knife) crosswise on the diagonal to 1/2" thick slices. Arrange the biscotti, cut sides down, on the cookie sheets and bake them for 6 to 8 minutes on each side or until they are a light golden brown.

Cool 1 minute, then remove from cookie sheets to wire racks to cool completely.

For the Icing: In a small bowl, whisk together the confectioners' sugar, zest, and lemon juice. Add additional lemon juice if necessary to reach desired spreading consistency.

Spread Icing over about half of one end of each cookie. Place cookies atop wire rack set over waxed paper until set. Makes about 3 dozen.

Dark Chocolate Chipped and Dipped Biscotti

Dip and dunk these biscotti often.

1 cup granulated sugar
²/₃ cup unsalted butter, room temperature
12 oz. bittersweet chocolate, finely chopped
3 large eggs
1 tsp. pure vanilla extract
2³/₄ cups plus 2 tbsp. unbleached, all-purpose flour, divided
2¹/₂ tsp. baking powder
¹/₄ tsp. salt
5 oz. semisweet chocolate, finely chopped

DIP

12 oz. semisweet chocolate, finely chopped
2 tbsp. shortening

Heat oven to 350 degrees.

Using an electric mixer, in a large bowl, beat together the sugar and butter until light and fluffy. Scrape down sides and bottom of bowl.

Add the bittersweet chocolate pieces, eggs, and vanilla, beating until well mixed. Scrape down sides and bottom of bowl.

Mix in the 2³/₄ cups of flour, baking powder, and salt. Stir in the chocolate pieces. Dough will be soft and sticky.

Divide dough in half. Sprinkle a large piece of foil with the additional flour. Shape dough, with lightly floured hands, into 2 (14") logs on foil. Remove from foil and place on ungreased cookie sheets. Flatten logs to a 2" width with your hands.

Bake for 22 to 25 minutes or just until set. Cool on cookie sheets on wire cooling racks for 15 minutes.

Reduce oven temperature to 300 degrees. Carefully place each log, one at a time, on a cutting board and cut into ¹/₂" slices. Arrange slices on prepared cookie sheets. Bake for 8 minutes. Turn slices and bake for an additional 9 to 14 minutes or until crisp, dry, and a light golden brown. Cool completely on a wire rack.

For the Dip: Melt the semisweet chocolate with the shortening in a small saucepan over very low heat, stirring until melted and smooth.

Tilt saucepan and dip biscotti to cover halfway in chocolate. Place on cooling rack atop waxed paper until set. Makes about 4 dozen.

Triple Chocolate Biscotti

Another biscotti from my first cookbook, No Reservations Required, this triple chocolate one uses cocoa, white chocolate, and bittersweet chocolate as its triple threat!

⅓ cup unsalted butter, room temperature
⅔ cup granulated sugar
¼ cup unsweetened cocoa powder, sifted
2 tsp. baking powder
2 large eggs
1¾ cups unbleached, all-purpose flour
4 oz. white chocolate, coarsely chopped
3 oz. bittersweet chocolate, coarsely chopped

BEV'S BITES
Biscotti may be frozen in an airtight container for up to 6 months.

Heat oven to 375 degrees. Line cookie sheets with parchment paper.

Using an electric mixer, in a large bowl, beat together the butter and sugar until light and fluffy. Scrape down sides and bottom of bowl.

Add the cocoa powder and baking powder and beat until combined. Mix in the eggs, beating until well blended. Scrape down sides and bottom of bowl.

Mix in the flour just until combined. Stir in the white chocolate pieces and the bittersweet chocolate pieces.

Divide dough in half. Working on a parchment-paper-lined baking sheet with floured hands, form each piece of dough into a flattish log—10" long by 2" wide.

Arrange the logs at least 4" apart on another parchment-paper-lined cookie sheet. Bake for 20 to 25 minutes or until a light golden brown. Let them cool on the baking sheet on a wire rack for 30 minutes.

Reduce oven temperature to 325 degrees.

Carefully remove the logs, one at a time, to a large cutting board. Cut the logs (with a serrated knife) crosswise on the diagonal to ½" thick slices. Arrange the biscotti, cut sides down, on ungreased cookie sheets and bake them for 7 to 9 minutes on each side or until they are crisp and dry. (Do not overbake.)

Cool 1 minute, then remove from cookie sheets to wire racks to cool completely. Makes about 2 dozen.

White Chocolate Ginger Biscotti

I'm crazy for biscotti in all its varied flavor profiles, and this version is always a favorite, a mixture of sweet and spicy in a pleasingly unexpected way!

½ cup unsalted butter, room temperature
¾ cup granulated sugar
2 large eggs
1 tsp. pure vanilla extract
2 cups unbleached, all-purpose flour
1½ tsp. baking powder
¼ tsp. salt
6 oz. white chocolate, finely chopped
¼ cup finely chopped crystallized ginger

Heat oven to 325 degrees. Line cookie sheets with parchment paper.

Using an electric mixer, in a large bowl, beat the butter and sugar until light and fluffy. Scrape down sides and bottom of bowl.

Beat in eggs and vanilla. Mix in flour, baking powder, and salt until blended. Scrape down sides and bottom of bowl.

Stir in the white chocolate pieces and ginger pieces.

Divide dough into 2 pieces. Working on a parchment-paper-lined baking sheet with floured hands, form each piece of dough into a flattish log—14" long by 1½" wide.

Arrange the logs at least 2" apart on another parchment-paper-lined cookie sheet.

Bake for 20 to 25 minutes or just until a light golden brown. Let them cool on the baking sheet on a wire rack for 10 minutes.

Carefully remove the logs, one at a time, to a large cutting board. Cut the logs (with a serrated knife) on the diagonal to ¾" thick slices. Arrange the biscotti, cut sides down, on the cookie sheets and bake them for 5 to 8 minutes on each side or until they are a light golden brown.

Cool 1 minute, then remove from cookie sheets to wire racks to cool completely. Makes about 3 dozen.

Hawaiian Macadamia Nut Biscotti

Hawaii is known for its macadamia nuts, and crisp twice-baked cookies have not escaped their traditional offerings.

1/2 cup kirsch
2 cups dried tart cherries, snipped into pieces
2 cups unsalted macadamia nuts, toasted
1/2 cup and 1/3 cup granulated sugar, divided
1/2 cup firmly packed light brown sugar
3/4 cup unsalted butter, room temperature
4 large egg whites
2 tsp. pure vanilla extract
3 cups unbleached, all-purpose flour
1 large egg, lightly beaten

BEV'S BITES

If you don't have an insulted cookie sheet, put one cookie sheet atop another before baking.

Short for kirschwasser, which literally translates as cherry water, kirsch is a cherry brandy that is made by using a method of double distillation. The black cherry is the fruit of choice for the fermentation and distillation process, producing a brandy that has a robust flavor without a hint of sweetness. This characteristic helps to set kirsch apart from cherry liqueur, which is usually very sweet.

No kirsch in the house? Water is an acceptable (but not as tasty) substitute in this recipe.

In a small saucepan, bring kirsch just to a simmer (do not boil). Place dried cherries in a medium bowl. Pour the warm kirsch over the dried cherries and soak for 1 hour. Drain well and lay cherries out on several sheets of paper towels to absorb any excess moisture.

Heat oven to 325 degrees. Line an insulated cookie sheet with parchment paper.

In a food processor, pulse the macadamia nuts until they are coarsely chopped. Set aside.

Using an electric mixer, in a large bowl, beat 1/2 cup of the granulated sugar, brown sugar, and butter until light and fluffy. Scrape down sides and bottom of bowl.

Beat in the egg whites and the vanilla until the mixture is well combined. Scrape down sides and bottom of bowl.

Mix in the flour, nuts, and dried cherries until blended. (Dough will be soft and sticky.)

Working on a sheet of floured waxed paper, shape the dough into 2 8" logs. Place onto the prepared cookie sheet, spacing 3" apart, and brush with the beaten egg. Sprinkle with the remaining 1/3 cup granulated sugar.

Bake for about 40 to 45 minutes in the bottom third of the oven until golden and firm to the touch. Let cool on the baking sheet on a wire rack for 30 minutes.

Carefully remove the logs, one at a time, to a large cutting board. Cut the logs (with a serrated knife) on the diagonal to 1/3" thick slices. Arrange the biscotti, cut sides down, on the cookie sheets and bake them for 10 minutes on each side or until they are a light golden brown.

Cool 1 minute, then remove from cookie sheets to wire racks to cool completely. Makes about 2 dozen.

Rosemary Biscotti

A savory version of a classic Italian twice-baked cookie, perfect with a fresh green salad, a hearty soup, or with a cheese course.

¼ cup unsalted butter, room temperature
2 tbsp. light olive oil
¼ cup granulated sugar
1 tbsp. finely chopped fresh rosemary
2 tsp. baking powder
¼ tsp. salt
2 large eggs
⅓ cup medium-grind cornmeal
1⅔ cups unbleached, all-purpose flour
Milk as needed for brushing dough

BEV'S BITES

I enjoy rosemary so much more when it's finely chopped; otherwise, I feel as if I'm eating pine needles!

Heat oven to 375 degrees.

Using an electric mixer, beat together the butter and olive oil until blended. Add the sugar, rosemary, baking powder, and salt, beating until combined. Scrape down sides and bottom of bowl.

Beat in eggs and blend in cornmeal and flour, mixing until combined. Scrape down sides and bottom of bowl.

Divide the dough in half. Working on a parchment-paper-lined baking sheet with floured hands, form each piece of dough into a flattish log—9" long by 1½" wide.

Arrange the logs at least 3" apart on an ungreased cookie sheet. Flatten slightly (to about 2" wide) then brush with milk.

Bake for 20 minutes or until a wooden toothpick inserted near the center comes out clean. Cool on baking sheet atop wire rack for 1 hour.

Reduce oven temperature to 325 degrees.

Carefully remove the logs, one at a time, to a large cutting board. Cut the logs (with a serrated knife) diagonally to ½" thick slices. Arrange the biscotti, cut sides down, on the cookie sheets and bake them for 10 to 12 minutes on each side or until they are a light golden brown.

Cool 1 minute, then remove from cookie sheets to wire racks to cool completely. Makes about 2 dozen.

The perfect change-of-pace biscotti.
This Rosemary Biscotti is a host's secret weapon when
served with a cheese platter or a hearty soup and salad dinner.

Cranberry Pistachio Biscotti

I've always adored pistachios, and the combination with dried cranberries is sensational. This recipe, from my first cookbook No Reservations Required, *is an adaptation of a biscotti tasted in The Strip District in Pittsburgh.*

2½ cups unbleached, all-purpose flour
1 cup granulated sugar
½ tsp. baking soda
½ tsp. baking powder
½ tsp. salt
3 large eggs
1 tsp. pure vanilla extract
1 cup dried cranberries
1 cup natural pistachio nuts, shelled
   and coarsely chopped
1 large egg combined with 1 tbsp. milk

Heat oven to 325 degrees.

In a large bowl, blend together the flour, sugar, baking soda, baking powder, and salt until combined. Add the eggs and vanilla, mixing until dough is formed.

Stir in the cranberries and pistachios.

Turn the dough out onto a lightly floured surface, knead it several times then halve it. Working on a parchment-paper-lined baking sheet with floured hands, form each piece of dough into a flattish log—12" long by 2" wide.

Arrange the logs at least 3" apart on another parchment-paper-lined cookie sheet. Whisk together the remaining egg and milk and brush the logs with the egg wash.

Bake the logs in the middle of the oven for 30 minutes, and then let them cool on the baking sheet on a wire rack for 10 minutes.

Carefully remove the logs, one at a time, to a large cutting board. Cut the logs (with a serrated knife) crosswise on the diagonal to ¾" thick slices. Arrange the biscotti, cut sides down, on the cookie sheets and bake them for 10 to 12 minutes on each side or until they are a light golden brown.

Cool 1 minute, then remove from cookie sheets to wire racks to cool completely. Makes about 2½ dozen.

Flavors of Tuscany Biscotti

The Province of Prato, in Italy, is known for these crunchy, light cantucci.

1³/₄ cups unbleached, all-purpose flour
1 cup granulated sugar
1 tsp. baking powder
¹/₄ tsp. salt
1 cup whole almonds, toasted
2 large eggs
¹/₂ tsp. pure almond extract

Heat oven to 375 degrees.

In a large mixing bowl, combine the flour, sugar, baking powder, and salt.

Pulse the almonds in a food processor just until ground. Stir nuts into flour mixture.

In a measuring cup, whisk together the eggs and almond extract. Add the egg mixture to the flour/nut mixture, stirring just until blended. Dough will be crumbly.

Turn dough out onto a lightly floured surface and knead until dough comes together. Divide dough into 2 portions. Working on a parchment-paper-lined baking sheet with floured hands, form each piece of dough into a flattish log—6" long by 1" thick.

Arrange the logs at least 6" apart on parchment-paper-lined cookie sheet. Bake for 25 minutes or until a light golden brown. Cool for 5 minutes on a wire rack.

Carefully remove the logs, one at a time, to a large cutting board. Cut the logs (with a serrated knife) crosswise on the diagonal to ¹/₂" thick slices. Arrange the biscotti, cut sides down, on the cookie sheets and bake them for 10 to 14 minutes.

Cool completely on a wire rack. Makes about 2 dozen.

A helping hand is always welcome when serving these Cinnamon and Walnut Rugelach.

Cinnamon and Walnut Rugelach

Cream cheese always makes for a delightfully rich dough, and here we've reduced the fat by using Neufchâtel cheese.

1 cup unsalted butter, room temperature
8 oz. Neufchâtel cheese, room temperature
½ cup granulated sugar
2¾ cups unbleached, all-purpose flour
1 tsp. salt

FILLING

¾ cup firmly packed light brown sugar
1⅓ cups finely chopped walnuts, toasted
½ cup unsalted butter, melted and cooled
1 tbsp. ground cinnamon
½ tsp. ground allspice

1 large egg, beaten to blend

BEV'S BITES
A pizza cutter is the perfect tool for cutting the wedges.

Leftover Filling? It can be stored, well wrapped, in the freezer for future use or crumbled atop your favorite muffin batter.

Using an electric mixer, in a large bowl beat, butter and cheese until light and fluffy. Scrape down sides and bottom of bowl.

Beat in sugar until blended. Mix in flour and salt. Gather the dough into a ball and mix gently until smooth. Divide the dough into 8 pieces and flatten into disks. Wrap in plastic wrap and chill 1 hour or up to overnight.

For the Filling: In a medium bowl, stir together the brown sugar, walnuts, butter, cinnamon, and allspice until well blended. Set aside.

Heat oven to 350 degrees. Roll dough out on a lightly floured surface to an 8" round, one disk at a time (keeping remaining dough refrigerated).

Spread about 3 tbsp. of Filling over round, leaving ½" border. Cut round into 8 wedges. Starting at wide end of each wedge, roll up tightly and completely to tip. Place cookies, tip down, on ungreased cookie sheets, curving gently to form into crescents. Repeat with remaining dough disks and Filling. Brush cookies with egg wash.

Bake for 15 to 20 minutes or until golden. Cool 1 minute, then remove from cookie sheets to wire racks to cool completely. Makes about 4½ dozen.

Crisp with Chips of Chocolate Shortbread

One taste of these and you might never buy another prepackaged shortbread cookie again!

¾ cup confectioners' sugar, sifted
¾ cup unsalted butter, room temperature
¾ tsp. pure vanilla extract
1⅓ cups unbleached, all-purpose flour
3 tbsp. cornstarch
⅛ tsp. salt
3 oz. semisweet or bittersweet chocolate, finely chopped
⅓ cup coarse grain sugar, such as turbinado

Heat oven to 350 degrees.

Using an electric mixer, in a large bowl, beat the confectioners' sugar, butter, and vanilla until light and fluffy. Scrape down sides and bottom of bowl.

Mix in the flour, cornstarch, and salt until blended. Stir in the chocolate pieces.

On a lightly floured surface, roll dough to a 10" square. Cut into 16 squares, and then diagonally cut each square in half.

Place each wedge 1½" apart onto ungreased cookie sheets. Sprinkle tops with coarse sugar.

Bake for 9 to 12 minutes or just until edges are a light golden brown. Makes 32 pieces.

Studs of White Chocolate and Cherry Shortbread

This shortbread is sensational . . . flavorful and colorful, it makes a beautiful addition to a cookie tray or a light but fancy dessert.

¼ cup maraschino cherries, well drained and finely chopped
¼ cup tart dried cherries, snipped into pieces
2½ cups unbleached, all-purpose flour
½ cup granulated sugar plus additional for dipping glass
1 cup unsalted butter, cold, cut into pieces
6 oz. white chocolate, finely chopped
1 tsp. pure vanilla extract

DIP

5 oz. white chocolate, finely chopped
2 tsp. shortening

Heat oven to 325 degrees. Spread cherries atop layers of paper towels to drain well. Lightly pat dry with additional paper towel just before using.

Using an electric mixer, in a large bowl, combine the flour and sugar. Mix in the butter just until it resembles fine crumbs.

Stir in the drained cherries, tart cherries, and the white chocolate pieces. Stir in the vanilla.

With lightly floured hands, gently knead the dough until it forms a smooth ball.

Shape dough into ¾" balls and place 1½" apart on ungreased cookie sheets. Press dough with bottom of a flat glass dipped in additional sugar, making 1½" rounds.

Bake for 10 to 12 minutes or until centers are set. Cool 1 minute, then remove from cookie sheets to wire racks to cool completely.

For the Dip: In a double boiler, set over barely simmering water, combine the white chocolate and the shortening. Stir until melted and smooth.

Dip half of each cookie into the white chocolate mixture, allowing excess to drip off. Place cookies on wire rack set atop sheets of waxed paper until chocolate is set. Makes about 3½ dozen.

Hazelnut Pecan Shortbread

Hazelnuts and pecans make for a rich and flavorful combination in this buttery shortbread recipe.

1 cup unsalted butter, room temperature
⅔ cup granulated sugar
½ cup finely ground pecans
½ cup finely ground hazelnuts
2 cups unbleached, all-purpose flour
¼ tsp. salt

BEV'S BITES

Once you've skinned and toasted the hazelnuts, grind them in a food processor or blender using a series of short pulses rather than the "on" switch. This will ensure a fine grind as opposed to nut butter!

Heat oven to 375 degrees.

Using an electric mixer, in a large bowl, beat together the butter and sugar until light and fluffy. Scrape down sides and bottom of bowl.

Stir in the nuts, mixing until well combined. Mix in the flour and salt, just until the dough holds together.

Roll the dough onto a lightly floured surface to ½" thick. Cut into simple shapes with a pizza cutter or cookie cutter and place the shapes on ungreased cookie sheets.

Bake for 8 to 12 minutes or just until a light golden brown on the bottom. Cool 1 minute, then remove from cookie sheets to wire racks to cool completely.

Makes about 3½ dozen (depending on size and shape).

Luck O' the Irish Oatmeal Shortbread

Perfect with a cup of Irish coffee or a morning spot of tea, this oatmeal version of a classic shortbread is delectable.

1 cup unbleached, all-purpose flour
3 tbsp. granulated sugar
$\frac{1}{2}$ cup unsalted butter, cut into
    pieces, cold
$\frac{1}{3}$ cup quick-cooking oats

Heat oven to 325 degrees.

In a medium bowl, combine the flour and sugar. Using a pastry blender or two forks, cut in the butter until mixture resembles fine crumbs and just starts to cling together.

Stir in the oats. Form mixture into a ball and knead gently, just until smooth.

On an ungreased cookie sheet, pat the dough into an 8" circle, making a decorative scalloped edge if you're feeling creative.

Using a pizza cutter or a sharp knife, cut the circle into 16 wedges, leaving wedges together.

Bake for 18 to 25 minutes or until bottom just starts to turn golden brown and center is set.

While still warm, cut circle into wedges again to separate. Cool 5 minutes, then remove from cookie sheet to wire racks to cool completely. Makes 16 pieces.

Hungarian Cream Cheese Kifli

These are the cookies of my childhood; every year during Easter or Christmas or for special celebrations huge quantities of these cookies would be made and filled with lekvar (prune butter), nut filling, or poppy seed filling. If I wanted apricot filling (which I dearly loved), I'd have to go to a friend's home.

1 lb. unsalted butter, cut into pieces, room temperature
1 lb. cream cheese, cut into pieces, room temperature
1 tbsp. baking powder
6 large egg yolks, reserving egg whites for brushing cookies
5 cups unbleached, all-purpose flour
Confectioners' sugar for dusting cookies

BEV'S BITES —————————

I prefer to roll the dough out on large round cloth-covered pastry board lightly dusted with a mix of half confectioners' sugar, sifted, and half unbleached, all-purpose flour. This mixture helps keep the dough tender.

For this to be enjoyable it really is a two person job—one to cut and fill, the other to fold and brush and place on cookie sheets.

Using an electric mixer, in a large bowl, cream together the butter and cream cheese until light and fluffy. Scrape down sides and bottom of bowl.

Mix the baking powder into egg yolks, whisking to blend. Add to the butter mixture, blending well.

Add the flour gradually until all is incorporated and dough comes away from bowl.

Divide dough in eighths and shape each into a disk. Wrap in plastic wrap; flatten to $\frac{1}{2}$". Chill dough overnight.

Heat oven to 350 degrees. Line cookies sheets with parchment paper.

Roll dough on lightly floured board, turning and flipping as you roll, until very thin, a minimum of $\frac{1}{16}$". Cut 2" squares (or any desired shape). Fill with $\frac{1}{2}$ tsp. to $\frac{3}{4}$ tsp. of desired filling and fold 2 of the opposite corners together. Pinch lightly to seal. Brush with reserved egg whites.

Bake until a light golden brown, about 20 minutes. Cool 1 minute, then remove from cookie sheets to wire racks to cool completely.

Sprinkle cookies with confectioners' sugar when cool. Makes about 12 dozen (recipe can easily be halved).

Rows of Apricot-Filled and Lekvar-Filled Hungarian Cream Cheese Kiflis with an antique sieve that belonged to my mom. (Note that a few Kiflis had to be eaten for quality-control purposes.)

"Milk Candy" Sandwich Cookies

My version of a caramel sensation, dulce de leche, with a coffee caramel twist. Use your favorite prepared thick caramel sauce for this delectable cookie.

1 cup unsalted butter, room temperature
²/₃ cup granulated sugar plus additional for dipping glass
2 large egg yolks
2 tbsp. dark rum
1 tbsp. plus 1 tsp. pure vanilla extract
2½ cups unbleached, all-purpose flour
1 tsp. baking powder
¼ tsp. salt
1 cup of purchased thick coffee caramel sauce or your favorite thick caramel sauce

BEV'S BITES

Dulce de leche in Spanish is a milk-based syrup, and is extremely popular across Latin America as both a sauce and a caramellike candy. I've used my version of this "milk candy" in this cookie . . . a thick, coffee caramel sauce that adds another flavor dimension. One of my cookie testers loved these cookies rolled in lightly toasted, flaked coconut, while another liked it rolled in chopped peanuts. Honestly, it's just as good when not rolled in anything!

Using an electric mixer, in a large bowl, beat together the butter and ²/₃ cup of the granulated sugar until light and fluffy. Add egg yolks, rum, and vanilla, beating until well blended. Scrape down sides and bottom of bowl.

Mix in flour, baking powder, and salt just until blended.

Cover and chill dough for 30 minutes.

Heat oven to 350 degrees. Line cookie sheets with parchment paper.

Shape dough into ¾" balls, and place 2" apart on prepared cookie sheets. Press dough with bottom of a flat glass dipped in additional sugar to make each about 1½" in diameter.

Bake for 10 to 12 minutes or just until edges turn a light golden brown. Cool 1 minute, then remove from cookie sheets to wire racks to cool completely.

For each sandwich cookie, spread about 1 tsp. of the coffee caramel sauce on the bottom of 1 cookie, spreading to the edge of the cookie. Top with a second cookie, bottom side in. Gently squeeze until filling JUST begins to ooze out a little around the edges. Makes about 2½ dozen.

Sugar Cookies from the Netherlands with White Chocolate Drizzle

A holiday tradition in the Netherlands, St. Nick gives all good Dutch children cookie cutouts along with their other gifts. Have you been good?

1½ cups confectioners' sugar, sifted
1 cup unsalted butter, room temperature
1 large egg
2 tsp. pure vanilla extract
2½ cups unbleached, all-purpose flour
1 tsp. baking powder
½ tsp. salt

DRIZZLE

4 oz. coarsely chopped white chocolate

BEV'S BITES

No pastry bag or tip? Use a quart-size Ziploc bag, pushing chocolate into one corner. With kitchen shears, snip a tiny piece off the corner of the bag and pipe as directed.

Using an electric mixer, in a large bowl, beat together the sugar and butter until light and fluffy. Beat in the egg and vanilla. Scrape down sides and bottom of bowl.

Mix in the flour, baking powder, and salt just until combined.

Divide dough in half and shape into 2 disks. Wrap in plastic wrap; flatten to ½". Chill dough for 2 hours.

Heat oven to 325 degrees.

Roll dough out on a lightly floured surface to ⅛" thick, one disk at a time (keeping remaining dough refrigerated). Cut with your favorite cookie cutters.

Transfer cutouts to ungreased cookie sheets, spacing 1" apart. Gather scraps, reroll, and cut.

Bake for 10 to 14 minutes or just until a pale golden color. Cool 1 minute, then remove from cookie sheets to wire racks to cool completely.

In a double boiler set over simmering (not boiling) water, melt the white chocolate, stirring often, just until smooth. Remove top of double boiler and place on kitchen towel.

Spoon melted chocolate into a pastry bag fitted with a ⅟₁₆" plain tip. Pipe chocolate onto cookies in a decorative fashion. Let cookies stand until chocolate sets. Makes about 3½ dozen depending on shapes used.

European Spice Wafers

Roll these cookies super thin for the most traditional flavor and texture.

6 tbsp. unsalted butter, room temperature
3/4 cup granulated sugar
1/4 cup molasses
1 large egg yolk
1 2/3 cups unbleached, all-purpose flour
    plus additional for rolling
1/2 tsp. salt
1/2 tsp. baking powder
1/4 tsp. baking soda
1 tsp. ground cinnamon
3/4 tsp. ground ginger
1/4 tsp. ground cloves
1 tsp. finely ground white pepper

Heat oven to 325 degrees.

Using an electric mixer, in a large bowl, beat together the butter, sugar, and molasses until light and fluffy. Scrape down sides and bottom of bowl.

Beat in the egg yolk. Mix in the flour, salt, baking powder, baking soda, cinnamon, ginger, cloves, and white pepper just until combined.

Place a large sheet of plastic wrap on a damp surface. Top with a quarter of the dough, pressing down to form a disk. Dust lightly with flour and top with another large sheet of plastic wrap.

Roll the dough until at least 1/16" (no thicker). Transfer the rolled dough to a baking sheet or large plate and freeze until firm and you can easily peel back the plastic wrap, at least 40 minutes. Repeat with the remaining dough.

Cut the dough using a 2" round cookie cutter and return them to the freezer to set for 1 to 2 hours; this keeps the cookies from spreading too much when they bake. (Cutouts may be stacked between small pieces of waxed paper in the freezer.) Transfer frozen cookies to cookie sheets lined with parchment paper.

Bake 8 to 10 minutes or until crisp and light colored. Cool 1 minute, then remove from cookie sheets to wire racks to cool completely. Makes about 4 dozen.

Florentines

Another childhood tradition in my family, these Italian classics are deceptively simple to make. My job was to drizzle them with chocolate.

1³/₄ cups sliced, blanched almonds
3 tbsp. unbleached, all-purpose flour
2 tbsp. fresh orange zest, finely grated
¹/₄ tsp. salt
³/₄ cup granulated sugar
2 tbsp. heavy (whipping) cream
2 tbsp. light corn syrup
5 tbsp. unsalted butter
¹/₂ tsp. pure vanilla extract
4 oz. semisweet chocolate, coarsely chopped

BEV'S BITES

Can't find blanched almonds? You can blanch them yourself by placing the almonds in a bowl and pouring boiling water to barely cover over the top. Let almonds sit for 1 minute. Drain, rinse under cold water, and drain again. Pat dry with a clean kitchen towel, slipping the skins off in the process. Toast in a dry skillet until almonds are fragrant, being careful not to burn.

So what's a rolling boil? A term often used in jelly making, a rolling boil refers to liquid that has reached a vigorous boiling point that cannot be stopped when stirred.

Heat oven to 350 degrees. Line cookie sheets with parchment paper.

In a food processor, pulse the almonds until finely chopped, being careful not to overdo it. In a large bowl, stir together the finely chopped almonds, flour, zest, and salt. Set aside.

In a small saucepan, combine the sugar, cream, corn syrup, and butter. Stir and cook over medium heat until mixture comes to a rolling boil and sugar is completely dissolved.

Continue to boil for 1 minute. Remove from heat and stir in the vanilla, then pour mixture into almond mixture, stirring just to combine. Set aside until cool enough to handle, usually about 30 minutes.

Scoop rounded teaspoonfuls (which will make generously sized 3" cookies) of batter and roll into balls. Place on prepared cookie sheets, leaving 3¹/₂" between each cookie (they spread).

Bake one cookie sheet at a time, for 9 to 11 minutes, in the middle of the oven. When done, cookies will be thin and an even golden brown color throughout. Rotate the cookie sheets halfway through baking time.

Cool 5 minutes, then remove from cookie sheets to wire racks to cool completely.

Place the semisweet chocolate in a double boiler over simmering water and stir until melted and smooth. Drizzle the melted chocolate over Florentines as desired. Keep on wire racks until chocolate is set. Makes about 3 dozen.

Amaretti

An Italian tradition, these little morsels are light as a feather and delicate with an intense sweet almond flavor.

2 large egg whites, room temperature
1 tbsp. Amaretto
½ tsp. pure vanilla extract
¼ tsp. cream of tartar
½ cup granulated sugar
2 tbsp. unbleached, all-purpose flour
1½ cups blanched, toasted, and finely
    ground almonds

BEV'S BITES

No Amaretto in the liqueur cabinet? Use ¼ tsp. almond extract instead.

So what are soft peaks? Once beaten to soft peaks, the tips of the egg whites will curl over.

And what are stiff peaks? These tips stand up straight and tall!

An egg separator is often times a kitchen luxury, but clean hands used to separate the eggs for these Amaretti cookies work well, too.

Heat oven to 300 degrees. Line cookie sheets with parchment paper.

Using an electric mixer, in a large bowl, beat the egg whites until frothy. Add the Amaretto, vanilla, and cream of tartar, then beat on medium-high speed until soft peaks form. Scrape down sides and bottom of bowl.

Slowly beat in the sugar, 1 tbsp. at a time, beating on high speed until stiff peaks form and sugar is almost dissolved. Beat in flour just until combined, then fold in almonds.

Quickly spoon whipped mixture into a pastry bag fitted with a ½" round tip. Pipe into 1" mounds, 1" apart on prepared cookie sheets.

Bake for 10 minutes or until crisp and set. Turn oven off. Let cookies remain in the closed oven for 30 minutes to dry out. Gently peel cookies from paper. Cool completely on a wire rack. Makes about 3½ dozen.

Italian Fig-Filled Cookies

My friend and fellow baker Annette Sarich makes these cookies from her Italian heritage, tweaked to her liking, often. They have a wonderfully figgy filling complemented by a bright citrus flavor.

1 cup unsalted butter, room temperature
1½ cups granulated sugar
4 large eggs, lightly beaten
4 tbsp. heavy (whipping) cream
2 tsp. pure vanilla extract
5 cups unbleached, all-purpose flour
½ tsp. baking soda
1 tsp. salt

FILLING

2 9 oz. packages dried figs
3½ cups water
1½ cups golden raisins
1½ cups coarsely ground almonds, toasted
¼ cup clover honey
2 tsp. fresh orange zest, finely grated
1½ tbsp. fresh orange juice
1 tsp. ground cinnamon
½ tsp. freshly grated nutmeg
¼ tsp. ground cloves

GLAZE

3 cups confectioners' sugar, sifted
2 tbsp. unsalted butter, melted
2 tsp. milk or more as needed to thin
1 cup coarsely chopped almonds

BEV'S BITES

Don't let these directions intimidate you. Once you get the rhythm of these cookies down, you'll be dancing the Tarantella between folds!

You'll have about 1 cup of the filling left. What to do? What to do? Smear it atop biscotti or toasted bread, or serve it with an assortment of Italian cheeses.

Using an electric mixer, in a large bowl, beat together the butter, sugar, and eggs until light and well blended. Scrape down sides and bottom of bowl.

Add in the cream and vanilla, beating to blend. Mix in the flour, baking soda, and salt until combined. Cover and chill dough for 30 minutes to 1 hour.

For the Filling: Cut and remove stems from dried figs. Place figs in a medium saucepan in 3½ cups of boiling water; remove from heat, cover, and let stand for 3 to 5 minutes. Strain figs (reserving fig water to use if necessary for thinning).

Place figs in a food processor and pulse until ground to a paste, adding a little of the fig water if necessary to smooth. Should make about 2½ cups fig paste.

Place raisins in food processor and grind to a paste, adding a little of the fig water if necessary to smooth.

In a medium bowl, combine the fig paste and raisin paste. Mix in the ground almonds, honey, orange zest, orange juice, cinnamon, nutmeg, and cloves. Stir to blend well, adding a little of the fig water if necessary to soften while mixing until desired consistency. Cover and chill until ready to assemble cookies.

Heat oven to 350 degrees.

Pinch off 1¼" size balls. Roll and flatten to a 2½" size disk. Fill with a heaping teaspoonful of Filling in the middle of the dough, folding over so edges meet. Pinch edges together.

With seam side down, pat the two ends to flatten slightly, then fold the ends under. Bake for 12 to 14 minutes or until golden on bottoms only. (Do not overbake or cookie dough will become dry.)

Cool 1 minute, then remove from cookie sheets to wire racks set atop waxed paper.

For the Glaze: In a medium bowl, whisk together the confectioners' sugar, melted butter, and the milk until blended. Add additional milk if necessary to reach desired Glaze consistency.

Spoon Glaze over still warm cookies. Top with a sprinkling of coarsely chopped almonds. Cool completely on wire rack until Glaze is set. Makes about 5 dozen.

Did they think we wouldn't notice that a bite was taken from this Italian Fig-Filled Cookie?

Italian Lemon Cookies

It's important not to overmix the dough for these cookies to ensure tender, flavorful results.

1½ cups granulated sugar
1 cup shortening
6 large eggs
½ cup milk
1½ tsp. pure vanilla extract
4 tbsp. pure lemon extract
6½ cups unbleached, all-purpose flour, divided
6 generous tsp. baking powder

GLAZE

1 lb. confectioners' sugar, sifted
2 to 3 tbsp. milk plus more as needed
1 tbsp. pure lemon extract

BEV'S BITES

Note that the tops of these cookies don't brown.

Heat oven to 350 degrees. Line cookie sheets with parchment paper.

Using an electric mixer, in a large bowl, beat together the sugar and shortening until blended. Add the eggs, milk, and vanilla and lemon extract, beating until combined. Scrape down sides and bottom of bowl.

In a small bowl, mix together 2 cups of the flour and the baking powder. Add to the egg mixture.

Add the remaining flour, a little at a time, stirring just to blend. Do not overmix.

Pinch off small pieces of dough and roll into 2" pieces. Fold dough in half (to form a tight "v" shape). Then braid the dough pieces, one half over the other.

Place on prepared sheets. Bake for 10 to 15 minutes or just until a light golden brown. Cool 1 minute, then remove from cookie sheets to wire racks to cool completely.

For the Glaze: In a medium bowl, whisk together the confectioners' sugar, 2 to 3 tbsp. of milk, and lemon extract, adding more milk as needed for desired brushing consistency.

Set wire rack over sheets of waxed paper. Brush Glaze atop cookies and allow to set. Makes about 5½ dozen.

Eastern European Mazurka Bars

A Russian and Polish heritage recipe with outstanding flavors. With a few variations, this is one of the tastiest versions I grew up with.

1 cup unsalted butter, room temperature
1 cup granulated sugar
1 large egg
1½ tsp. pure vanilla extract
2 cups unbleached, all-purpose flour
½ tsp. baking powder
¼ tsp. salt

FILLING

4 tsp. cornstarch
4 tsp. granulated sugar
1 cup fresh orange juice
½ cup dried apricots, snipped into pieces
½ cup pitted dates, snipped into pieces
¼ cup dried cherries, snipped into pieces
¼ cup seedless raisins
2 tbsp. fresh orange zest, finely grated
¾ cup roasted, shelled pistachios
1 tsp. fresh lemon zest, finely grated

Heat oven to 375 degrees. Lightly grease a 13x9" baking pan, then line the bottom of the pan with parchment paper.

Using an electric mixer, in a large bowl, beat together the butter and sugar until light and fluffy. Scrape down sides and bottom of bowl.

Add the egg and vanilla, beating until well combined. Mix in the flour, baking powder, and salt. Scrape down sides and bottom of bowl.

Evenly spread the mixture into the prepared pan. Bake for 22 to 30 minutes or until a golden brown. Cool completely on a wire rack.

For the Filling: In a 2-qt. saucepan, whisk together the cornstarch and sugar; blend in the orange juice until sugar dissolves.

Stir in the fruit pieces and orange zest. Bring to a simmer over medium heat, stirring often. Continue cooking and stirring until mixture thickens, about 10 additional minutes.

Heat oven to 350 degrees.

Remove the saucepan from the heat and stir in the pistachios and lemon zest. Spread Filling evenly over the top of the cooled crust.

Return pan to the oven and bake until golden brown around the edges and the Filling is just beginning to set, about 12 minutes. Cool completely on a wire rack.

Cut using a nonstick or lightly greased knife. Makes about 2 dozen.

Butter Press Cookies

I've always loved those round spritz press cookies, topped with colorful sprinkles or with a half of a glacé cherry perfectly positioned right in the middle. Here's a recipe that's perfect for your next cookie tray.

½ cup sliced, blanched almonds, toasted
¾ cup granulated sugar
1 cup unsalted butter, room temperature
1 large egg
2 tsp. pure vanilla extract
2 cups unbleached, all-purpose flour
Pinch of salt
Glacé cherries, halved
Sugar sprinkles

BEV'S BITES

Cookie Press 101: To get the best possible shape, hold the press so that the tube is straight up with the toothed edge just barely touching the cookie sheet. Squeeze firmly without moving it until the shape is as wide as you desire. Stop squeezing and push down just slightly on the plunger. Lift straight up and away.

Heat oven to 375 degrees.

Place the almonds on a jellyroll pan and bake them, stirring occasionally, for about 5 minutes or just until lightly browned. Cool completely on a wire rack.

In a food processor, pulse the almonds until they are finely ground. Set aside.

Using an electric mixer, in a large bowl, beat the sugar and butter until light and fluffy. Add the egg and vanilla and beat until blended. Scrape down sides and bottom of bowl.

Beat in the flour, salt, and ground almonds until well blended.

Scoop the dough into a cookie press with your favorite disk attached, and pipe onto ungreased cookie sheets spacing 1½" apart.

Decorate with cherry halves or sprinkles. Bake for 10 to 12 minutes or until a pale golden color. Cool 1 minute, then remove from cookie sheets to wire racks to cool completely.
Makes about 3 dozen.

Lemon Pizzelles

Having tasted traditional pizzelles for many years, my taste buds came alive when I bit into the crisp, lemon-scented pizzelles made by Josephine Smalley at one of my speaking engagements at a traveling Smithsonian exhibit. Here's my version of that delightful treat.

6 large eggs
$\frac{1}{2}$ cup vegetable oil
2 tsp. pure lemon extract
3 cups unbleached, all-purpose flour
2 tsp. baking powder
$1\frac{1}{2}$ cups granulated sugar

BEV'S BITES

Pizzelle makers just keep getting easier to use. My personal favorite is the Pizzelle Pro (the box says it "makes 3 party-size pizzelles") by Chef's Choice. It's quick and easy to use and has a latch so it stays together after the batter is added to keep pizzelles uniformly thin.

In a large bowl, whisk the eggs until smooth. Add the oil and lemon extract, whisking until blended.

Sift the flour and baking powder atop the egg mixture. Add the sugar and vigorously blend together into the egg mixture until smooth. The mixture will be sticky and stiff.

Heat pizzelle maker. Test by dropping the mixture from a small tsp. If needed, add a few tablespoonfuls of water so that the mixture drops as a ribbon in 2 to 3 seconds. If the mixture is too thin, add a few tablespoonfuls of flour. Bake until crisp and done. Makes about 100 (party size!).

Luscious Linzer Cookies

One peek at these cookies and you'll recognize some similarities to a Linzer Torte. Traditionally linzer cookies are filled with black currant preserves, but these are filled with red raspberry fruit spread or jam.

1½ cups unsalted butter, room temperature
1¾ cup confectioners' sugar, sifted, divided
1 large egg
2 cups unbleached, all-purpose flour
1 cup cornstarch
2 cups walnuts, finely ground
⅔ cup red raspberry fruit spread or jam

A mini diamond cookie cutter cuts the perfect shape, allowing a raspberry filling to peek through the top of this Luscious Linzer Cookie.

Using an electric mixer, in a large bowl, beat together the butter and 1 cup of the confectioners' sugar until light and fluffy. Scrape down sides and bottom of bowl.

Add the egg, mixing well. In a medium bowl, whisk together the flour and cornstarch then blend into the butter mixture until well combined. Scrape down sides and bottom of bowl.

Mix in the ground walnuts. Divide dough in half and shape into 2 disks. Wrap in plastic wrap; flatten to ½". Chill dough for 2 hours or up to overnight.

Heat oven to 325 degrees. Roll dough out on a lightly floured surface to ¼" thick, one disk at a time (keeping remaining dough refrigerated). Cut with a 2" round cookie cutter and place on ungreased cookie sheets.

Gather scraps, reroll, and cut additional cookies. For half the cookies, cut out a small diamond or round pattern from the middle with a mini cookie cutter.

Bake for 12 to 14 minutes or just until they are a light golden. Cool 1 minute, then remove from cookie sheets to wire racks to cool completely.

Place wire racks over waxed paper and generously sprinkle the remaining ¾ cup confectioners' sugar over the cookie tops with the cut outs. Spread each solid cookie with about ¼ tsp. of the fruit spread or jam. Top each cookie with a cookie top, sugared side out, pressing gently together. Makes about 4 dozen.

Sprinkled Danish Wreaths

*This cookie is a family affair. Pipe the dough and let others shape
into cookie wreaths, sneaking a bite or two as they go!*

4 cups unbleached, all-purpose flour
1½ cups plus 2 tbsp. unsalted butter,
   cut into pieces, cold
1 tsp. pure vanilla extract or vanilla
   bean paste
⅔ cup granulated sugar
1 large egg
1 tbsp. milk, whole or 2 percent
3 oz. almond paste
Assorted colorful sprinkles

BEV'S BITES

Almond paste is typically made from
ground almonds, sugar, glycerin, and
almond extract.

In my Chunks of Chocolate Cookies
recipe, I refer to vanilla bean paste that
can be used in place of splitting vanilla
beans. It's a wonderful trick-of-the-trade
ingredient to have on hand.

Using an electric mixer, in a large bowl, beat together the flour
and butter until coarse crumbs form.

Add the vanilla or vanilla bean paste, sugar, egg, milk, and
almond paste, beating to form a firm dough.

Cover and chill dough for 2 hours (up to overnight) to allow flavors to meld together.

Heat oven to 350 degrees. Line cookie sheets with parchment
paper.

Bring dough to room temperature. Spoon the dough into a pastry bag lined with a ½" to 1" star tip. Pipe a length of dough
about 4" long.

Transfer the piece of dough to a prepared cookie sheet, forming
into a circle and gently pinching the ends together. Space the circles about ¾" apart. Sprinkle with the sprinkles.

Bake for 7 to 11 minutes or just until firm and golden around
the edges. Makes about 4½ dozen.

Swiss Leckerle

Loaded with citrus flavors, this sweet chewy cookie from Switzerland is more like a confectionery treat.

2½ cups unbleached, all-purpose flour
1 cup granulated sugar
1 cup toasted almonds, finely chopped
¼ cup candied orange peel, finely chopped
⅓ cup candied lemon or grapefruit peel, finely chopped
1 tsp. baking powder
1 tsp. ground cinnamon
¾ tsp. freshly grated nutmeg
¼ tsp. ground cloves
¾ cup honey, clover or orange blossom
2 tsp. pure vanilla extract
1 large egg

GLAZE

1 cup confectioners' sugar, sifted
½ tsp. fresh orange zest, finely grated
2 tsp. fresh orange juice plus additional as needed

BEV'S BITES

You can make your own candied orange, lemon, or grapefruit peel by blanching large strips of citrus zest in boiling water for 2 minutes to soften. Drain, pat dry, and immediately dredge in a shallow bowl of granulated sugar, coating all sides. Place on waxed paper to dry completely, then chop according to recipe. You should be able to find a good source of candied peel if making your own is too crafty for you.

Heat oven to 350 degrees. Line cookie sheets with parchment paper.

Using an electric mixer, in a large bowl, combine the flour, sugar, almonds, candied citrus peels, baking powder, cinnamon, nutmeg, and cloves, mixing well to blend.

In a small bowl, whisk together the honey, vanilla, and egg. Pour the honey mixture into the flour mixture, stirring until it forms a ball. Divide dough in half.

Roll dough out on a lightly floured surface, one half at a time, to ¼" thick. Using a pizza cutter or sharp knife, cut dough into 2x1" strips.

Place strips ½" apart on prepared cookie sheets. Bake for 9 to 12 minutes or just until a light golden brown. Cool 1 minute, then remove from cookie sheets to wire racks to cool for 15 minutes.

For the Glaze: In a small bowl, whisk together the confectioners' sugar, zest, and juice. Add enough additional orange juice (2 tsp. or more) to make a glaze you can brush atop warm strips.

Set wire rack atop sheets of waxed paper, then brush the cookie strips with the Glaze. Makes about 4½ dozen.

Orange Madeleines with White Chocolate Glaze and Bev's Raspberry Dust

I love this version of an orange-scented Madeleine, with a smattering of pecans, a sweet white chocolate glaze, and the tart burst of my raspberry dust! Yum!

MADELEINE

2 large eggs, yolks and whites separated
1/2 cup granulated sugar
1/2 cup unsalted butter, melted and cooled
1/2 tsp. fresh orange zest, finely grated
1 tbsp. fresh orange juice
1/2 tsp. pure vanilla extract
1/2 cup unbleached, all-purpose flour
1/2 tsp. baking powder
1/8 tsp. baking soda
1/8 tsp. salt
1/4 cup finely chopped pecans, toasted

BEV'S RASPBERRY DUST

2 to 4 oz. dried raspberries
1 tsp. to 1 tbsp. superfine sugar

8 oz. white chocolate, coarsely chopped

BEV'S BITES

I don't have many items in silicone bakeware, but I swear by my silicone Madeleine molds. They're a breeze to use and the finished cookie just pops right out!

Dried raspberries? I use the Just Tomatoes brand of dried fruit, in this case Just Raspberries. They're a nationally known brand of dried fruits and veggies (started out as Just Tomatoes). They add absolutely nothing to the process of drying their fruits and veggies; they simply take the water out and leave intense flavor behind.

Heat oven to 375 degrees. Grease and flour 24 3" Madeleine molds, or if using silicone, simply wipe each mold lightly with an oiled paper towel.

For the Madeleines: Using an electric mixer, in a medium bowl, beat together the egg yolks and sugar. Add the butter, zest, juice, and vanilla, beating until combined.

In a small bowl, stir together the flour, baking powder, baking soda, and salt. Sprinkle flour mixture over the yolk mixture, stirring gently to combine. Add the pecans.

With a whisk, lightly beat the egg whites in a clean medium bowl. Gently fold into batter, then spoon batter into prepared molds, filling each about half full.

Bake for 10 to 12 minutes or until edges are golden and tops spring back when lightly touched. Cool 1 minute, then remove from molds to wire racks to cool completely.

For the Dust: Purée the dried raspberries and sugar in a blender until smooth. Strain to remove seeds. Sprinkle atop plate for dipping. Leftovers must be stored in an airtight container at room temperature. Keeps about 1 month. Makes about 1 to 1 1/4 cups.

Melt white chocolate in a double boiler over a pot of simmering water, stirring just until smooth. Remove double boiler from atop water and set on towel.

Line cookie sheets with waxed paper. Dip the flat end of each Madeleine in the white chocolate, allowing excess to drip back into the double boiler top, then press into Bev's Berry Dust until white chocolate is lightly coated. Place on waxed paper and let dry. Makes about 2 dozen.

Had I known there was one Orange Madeleine with White Chocolate
Glaze and Bev's Raspberry Dust left, I would have eaten it immediately. The result? No photo!

Luscious Lemon Madeleines

The perfect Madeleine—made tender with cake flour, rich with egg yolks, and fresh with hints of lemon. Perfect with fresh fruit sorbet.

3 large eggs
2 large egg yolks
³/₄ cup granulated sugar
1 tsp. pure vanilla extract
2 tbsp. fresh lemon zest, finely grated
2 tbsp. fresh lemon juice
³/₄ cup unsalted butter, melted and cooled
1¹/₂ cups cake flour, sifted
¹/₂ tsp. baking powder
¹/₄ tsp. salt
¹/₃ cup confectioners' sugar, sifted

These Luscious Lemon Madeleines are my "go to" cookie for summer entertaining because they're perfect served on their own, with fresh fruit sorbet, or a big bowl of summer fruit salad.

Heat oven to 350 degrees. Grease and flour 24 3" Madeleine molds, or if using silicone, simply wipe each mold lightly with an oiled paper towel.

Using an electric mixer, in a large bowl, beat together the eggs, egg yolks, sugar, vanilla, zest, and lemon juice on medium-high speed until pale yellow and thickened. Drizzle in the melted butter and stir in the flour, baking powder, and salt.

Let batter set for 15 minutes, then spoon into prepared molds filling each about half full.

Bake for 9 to 10 minutes or until edges are golden and tops spring back when lightly touched. Cool 1 minute, then remove from molds to wire racks to cool completely.

Sprinkle with confectioners' sugar and serve. Makes 2 dozen.

Mini Apple Butter Bear Claws

Apple butter is almost as American as apple pie. These mini claws get their down-home flavor from apple butter, and would be perfect with a mug of hot spiced apple cider.

⅔ cup unsalted butter, room temperature
1 cup granulated sugar
1 tsp. baking powder
¼ tsp. salt
2 large eggs
1 tsp. pure vanilla extract
3 cups unbleached, all-purpose flour
1 cup apple butter

TOPPING

2 tbsp. granulated sugar
½ tsp. ground cinnamon
1 large egg
1 tbsp. water

Using an electric mixer, in a large bowl, beat together the butter and sugar until light and fluffy. Add the baking powder and salt, stirring to blend. Scrape down sides and bottom of bowl.

Beat in 2 eggs and vanilla until combined. Mix in the flour just until blended. Scrape down sides and bottom of bowl.

Divide dough in half and shape into 2 small rectangles. Wrap in plastic wrap. Chill dough for 2 hours.

Heat oven to 375 degrees. Line cookie sheets with parchment paper.

Roll dough out on a lightly floured surface to a 12" square, one piece at a time (keeping remaining dough refrigerated). Cut dough into 16 3" squares.

Spread about 1½ tsp. of the apple butter down the middle of each square. Resist the temptation to overfill or the apple butter will ooze out! Fold one edge of the dough over the filling. Fold over the other edge.

Place on prepared cookie sheets and make 3 slits halfway through dough on each cookie. Curve cookies slightly to separate cuts.

For the Topping: In a small bowl, stir together the sugar and cinnamon. In another small bowl, beat the remaining egg with 1 tbsp. of water until blended. Brush cookies lightly with egg mixture, then sprinkle with cinnamon sugar mixture.

Bake for 10 to 12 minutes or until golden brown. Cool 1 minute, then remove from cookie sheets to wire racks to cool completely. Makes about 2½ dozen.

If a grizzly bear comes around looking for this Mini Apple Butter Bear Claw, I wouldn't fight him for it. (There's more in the freezer.)

Hermits Down South

A traditional Southern favorite, these spicy pecan- and raisin-filled cookies will surely become a favorite of yours as well.

¾ cup unsalted butter, room temperature
¾ cup firmly packed light brown sugar
1 tsp. ground cinnamon
½ tsp. baking soda
¼ tsp. ground cloves
¼ tsp. ground nutmeg
1 large egg
¼ cup brewed espresso or other strong
   coffee, cooled
1½ cups unbleached, all-purpose flour
2 cups seedless raisins
1 cup coarsely chopped pecans, toasted

Heat oven to 375 degrees.

Using an electric mixer, in a large bowl, beat together the butter and brown sugar until light and fluffy. Scrape down sides and bottom of bowl.

Mix in the cinnamon, baking soda, cloves, and nutmeg. Beat in the egg and espresso just until blended. Scrape down sides and bottom of bowl.

Mix in flour, then stir in raisins and pecans.

Drop dough by generous tablespoonfuls 2" apart (cookies spread!) on ungreased cookie sheets. Bake for 9 to 11 minutes or just until edges are a light golden brown.

Cool 1 minute, then remove from cookie sheets to wire racks to cool completely. Makes about 3½ dozen.

Apricot Fingers or Butterhorns

These flavorful cookies are a cookie tray favorite of my friend and fellow cook Vickie Getz. Adding a touch of shortening makes the cookies flaky.

APRICOT FILLING

16 oz. dried apricots
6 tbsp. granulated sugar

FINGERS OR BUTTERHORNS

1 cup unsalted butter, room temperature
2 cups unbleached, all-purpose flour
1 large egg, separated
1 tbsp. shortening
1 cup sour cream

Granulated sugar

BEV'S BITES

If left on the original cookie sheets, the sugar will form a crust, melting around them, and you will be unable to get the cookies off the tray without crumbling.

Heat oven to 375 degrees.

For the Apricot Filling: Put the dried apricots in a medium saucepan. Cover with water and cook until soft and the water is absorbed. (Be careful not to burn.) Cool and purée in a blender until consistency reaches a very thick paste. Mix in the sugar. Set aside.

For the Fingers: In a large bowl, cut the butter into the flour with a butter knife or pastry blender until particles are the size of small peas. Make a "nest" in the middle and put 1 egg yolk in the "nest."

Mix in the shortening. Add the sour cream and mix thoroughly.

Knead gently with hands until all flour disappears. Divide dough into 4 pieces.

Roll dough, one piece at a time, out onto a floured board to ¼" thick. Cut into 3" squares.

Put Filling, by teaspoonful, in each square and roll up. Place seam side down on cookie sheets.

Lightly beat egg white, then brush on each cookie and sprinkle with granulated sugar, very, very liberally.

Transfer them to another cookie sheet before baking. Bake for 10 minutes or just until golden brown. Makes about 3½ dozen.

Poppy Seed Bars

My mom adored anything poppy seed, and she would always obtain it fresh and have it ground before using it. Her poppy seed fillings always contained fresh lemon zest.

FILLING

1½ cups poppy seeds
½ cup sliced and toasted almonds
1 tbsp. fresh lemon zest, finely grated
1 cup granulated sugar
⅔ cup milk, whole or 2 percent
4 tsp. fresh lemon juice
4 tbsp. unsalted butter, room temperature

CRUST/TOPPING

2 cups unbleached, all-purpose flour
1 cup confectioners' sugar, sifted plus
   additional for dusting bars
2 tsp. baking powder
½ cup sliced and toasted almonds
1 cup unsalted butter, cut into pieces,
   cold
1 large egg

For the Filling: Combine the poppy seeds, almonds, and zest in a food processor. Pulse until fine.

Transfer the mixture to a medium saucepan. Add the sugar, milk, lemon juice, and butter. Cook over medium heat, stirring often, until the mixture boils and thickens to a syrup. Remove from heat and cool.

Heat oven to 350 degrees. Lightly grease a 13x9" pan.

For the Crust: Combine the flour, confectioners' sugar, baking powder, and almonds in a food processor. Pulse to blend.

Sprinkle in the butter pieces and pulse until mixture resembles coarse crumbs. With the machine running, add the egg through the feed tube. Pulse until the dough just forms a ball.

Divide dough in half. With lightly floured hands, pat half of the dough onto the bottom of the prepared pan. Pour the cooled filling over the crust.

Crumble the remaining dough over the filling to create the Topping. Bake for 45 to 60 minutes or until the topping is golden brown.

Cool completely on a wire rack. Cut into bars. Makes about 3½ dozen.

CELEBRATION COOKIES

Wouldn't these Twinkling Lemon Cutouts be perfect to leave for the fat (sorry—jolly, rotund) man in the red suit or anyone else who has the nerve to climb down your chimney?

What's to celebrate?

Often times it's simply the celebration of getting up in the morning! Could it be the anticipation of a new baby's arrival, an upcoming wedding, or the bright future ahead for a new graduate. Maybe it's time to celebrate a recovery from an illness, family members gathered together for a holiday tradition, afternoon tea with not forgotten but seldom seen friends, or perhaps it's just time to celebrate wanting a cookie!

Twinkling Lemon Cutouts

Cut with a ruffled fan-shaped cookie cutter, these are beautiful cookies. An added bonus, they taste as good as they look.

1 cup granulated sugar
1 cup unsalted butter, room temperature
3 tbsp. milk, whole or 2 percent
2 tsp. fresh lemon zest, finely grated
1 large egg
3 cups unbleached, all-purpose flour
1½ tsp. baking powder
½ tsp. salt
Crushed sugar cubes or sparkling, colorful sugar sprinkles

Using an electric mixer, in a large bowl, beat the sugar and butter until light and fluffy. Scrape down sides and bottom of bowl.

Add milk, zest, and egg; blend well.

Mix in flour, baking powder, and salt. Scrape down sides and bottom of bowl.

Divide dough in half and shape into 2 disks. Wrap in plastic wrap; flatten to ½". Chill dough for 2 hours.

Heat oven to 375 degrees. Roll dough out on a lightly floured surface to ⅛" thick, one disk at a time (keeping remaining dough refrigerated).

Cut with your favorite cookie cutters, placing 1" apart on ungreased cookie sheets. Sprinkle with sugar. Bake for 7 to 9 minutes or just until edges are a light golden color.

Cool 1 minute, then remove from cookie sheets to wire racks to cool completely. Makes about 5½ dozen.

Peppermint White Chocolate Cutout Cookies

These are festive and fun and would be perfect cut into many other winter shapes—snowflakes, snowmen, and trees.

⅓ cup shortening
⅓ cup unsalted butter, room temperature
¾ cup granulated sugar
1 tsp. baking powder
1 large egg
2 tbsp. milk, whole or 2 percent
1 tsp. pure vanilla extract
⅓ cup unsweetened cocoa powder, sifted
1¾ cups unbleached, all-purpose flour
4 oz. white chocolate, coarsely chopped
1 tbsp. shortening
⅔ cup finely crushed peppermint candy

BEV'S BITES

Crushing peppermint candy is easy—a Ziploc bag, air pressed out and tightly sealed, and a rolling pin will do the trick nicely. Had a bad day? A hammer works, too!

Using an electric mixer, in a large bowl, beat together the shortening and butter until well mixed. Add the sugar, baking powder, egg, milk, and vanilla, beating until combined. Scrape down sides and bottom of bowl.

Mix in the cocoa powder and flour. Divide dough in half and shape into 2 disks. Wrap in plastic wrap; flatten to ½". Chill dough for 2 hours (up to overnight).

Heat oven to 375 degrees. Roll dough out on a lightly floured surface to ⅛ to ¼" thick, one disk at a time (keeping remaining dough refrigerated). Cut with a selection of your favorite cookie cutters, placing 1" apart on ungreased cookie sheets.

Bake for 6 to 9 minutes or just until firm to the touch and light golden. Cool 1 minute, then remove from cookie sheets to wire racks to cool completely.

In a double boiler, set over simmering (not boiling) water, melt the white chocolate and shortening, stirring often, just until smooth. Remove top of double boiler and place on kitchen towel.

Set wire racks over sheets of waxed paper, then drizzle (or dip) white chocolate over cookies. Sprinkle with crushed candy. Let cookies stand until chocolate is set. Makes about 2½ dozen.

Eggnog Cutouts

All the flavors of a cup of eggnog in cookie form . . . festive and tasty. Make these often, even without the holiday celebration.

2 cups unbleached, all-purpose flour
¾ cup granulated sugar
¾ tsp. baking powder
¾ tsp. freshly grated nutmeg
⅔ cup unsalted butter, cut into pieces, cold
1 large egg
2 tbsp. milk, whole or 2 percent

CONFECTIONERS' SUGAR ICING

1 cup confectioners' sugar, sifted
2 to 3 tsp. milk, whole or 2 percent

In a food processor, place the flour, sugar, baking powder, and nutmeg and pulse to combine.

Add cold pieces of butter and pulse several times just until the mixture forms fine crumbs.

In a small bowl, whisk together the egg and milk and add to the flour mixture. Pulse just until mixture is moistened. Divide dough in half and shape into 2 disks. Wrap in plastic wrap; flatten to ½". Chill dough for 2 hours.

Heat oven to 375 degrees. Line cookie sheets with parchment paper.

Roll dough out on a lightly floured surface to ⅛" thick, one disk at a time (keeping remaining dough refrigerated). Cut with your favorite cookie cutters, placing 1" apart on prepared cookie sheets.

Bake for 7 to 9 minutes or just until edges are a light golden color. Cool 1 minute, then remove from cookie sheets to wire racks to cool completely.

For the Icing: In a medium bowl, whisk together the confectioners' sugar and milk to make Icing desired spreading or piping consistency.

Decorate cooled cookies by spreading or, with a pastry bag and a thin tip, piping with the Icing. Makes about 2 dozen.

Once you've tasted them, it's hard to forget the sweet dried fruit flavors of these Visions of Sugar Plums dancing in your mouth.

Visions of Sugar Plums

The flavors of these cookies will truly dance in your head after one bite! A no-bake cookie that improves with age, they're easy to do ahead, reroll in confectioners' sugar and serve in decorative papers.

2 cups unsalted whole almonds, toasted
¼ cup plus 1 tbsp. honey, clover,
    orange blossom, or a favorite artisan
    honey
2 tsp. fresh orange zest, finely grated
1½ tsp. ground cinnamon
½ tsp. ground allspice
½ tsp. freshly grated nutmeg
1 cup finely snipped dried apricots
1 cup finely snipped pitted dates
Confectioners' sugar, sifted

Using a food processor, pulse the almonds until finely chopped (being careful not to over process and make almond butter!).

In a large bowl, combine the honey, zest, cinnamon, allspice, and nutmeg, mixing to blend well.

Stir in the ground almonds, apricots, and dates; mix well.

Press a tablespoonful of mixture into a small cookie scoop to form a ball. Roll in confectioners' sugar, then refrigerate, layered in an airtight container between sheets of waxed paper. Makes about 4½ dozen.

BEV'S BITES

Toast the almonds on the stovetop over medium-low heat in a dry skillet just until fragrant. Remove from skillet to a large plate and allow to cool before chopping.

Kitchen shears (everyone needs a pair) work well, dipped often in warm water, for snipping the apricots and dates into small pieces.

Wouldn't these make a wonderful gift from your kitchen?

Spice Things Up Three Pepper Cookies

Created for a "Spice Things Up with Pepper" cooking class, these cookies are spectacular with a substantial salad (forgoing the usual crackers).

½ cup unsalted butter, room temperature
1 cup granulated sugar
1½ tsp. baking powder
½ tsp. finely ground white pepper
½ tsp. finely ground black pepper
½ tsp. ground ginger
½ tsp. ground cloves
½ tsp. ground cinnamon
¼ tsp. ground cayenne pepper
1 large egg
1 tbsp. milk, whole or 2 percent
2 cups unbleached, all-purpose flour
Medium-grind black pepper
9½ oz. bittersweet chocolate, coarsely
    chopped
1 tbsp. shortening

Using an electric mixer, in a large bowl, beat the butter and sugar until light and fluffy. Scrape down sides and bottom of bowl.

Add the baking powder, white pepper, black pepper, ginger, cloves, cinnamon, and cayenne pepper, mixing until blended. Scrape down sides and bottom of bowl.

Beat in the egg and milk until combined. Mix in the flour until blended.

Shape each half of dough into 2 6½" logs and roll on 2 long sheets of waxed paper or plastic wrap. Twist the ends to seal the cylinders of dough. Chill the dough for 4 hours up to overnight.

Heat oven to 375 degrees.

Unwrap one log at a time and cut into ¼" thick slices, placing 2" apart on ungreased cookie sheets. Sprinkle cookies with a grind or two of black pepper, then bake for 8 to 9 minutes or just until edges are a light golden brown.

Cool 1 minute, then remove from cookie sheets to wire racks to cool completely.

In a double boiler, set over simmering (not boiling) water, melt the chocolate and shortening, stirring often, just until smooth. Remove top of double boiler and place on kitchen towel.

Dip each cookie halfway in melted chocolate, shaking off excess. Place cookies on a waxed-paper-lined cookie sheet. Let stand until chocolate is set. Makes about 4 dozen.

*If you've never had chocolate and pepper together before,
these Spice Things Up Three Pepper Cookies will convince
you that this combination is a winner.*

Cocoa Bittersweet Meringues

Chocolaty, crisp, sugary, and delish . . . a celebration in every bite!

1/4 cup unsweetened cocoa powder, sifted
3/4 cup plus 2 tbsp. confectioners' sugar, sifted
3 large egg whites, room temperature
1/4 tsp. cream of tartar
6 tbsp. granulated sugar
1 cup finely chopped bittersweet chocolate

BEV'S BITES

That's right, 200 degrees for 2 hours produces a crisp meringue that's sure to please.

There's only one way to keep these crisp—store in airtight containers.

Crisp and chocolaty best describes this Cocoa Bittersweet Meringue. (Note: This is not what I mean by "two eggs, separated!")

Heat oven to 200 degrees. Line cookie sheets with parchment paper.

Resift the cocoa powder and confectioners' sugar into a small bowl. Set aside.

Using an electric mixer, in a large bowl, beat the egg whites with cream of tartar until frothy. Scrape down sides and bottom of bowl.

With mixer running, gradually add the cocoa mixture and sugar to the egg whites, a little at a time. Beat on high for 1 minute. Scrape down sides and bottom of bowl.

Continue beating until stiff peaks form. Gently fold in the chocolate pieces.

Drop the mixture by generously rounded tablespoonfuls (a cookie scoop works well for size consistency) onto the prepared cookie sheets, placing 1½" apart.

Bake for 2 hours. Cookies will be crisp on the outside and slightly chewy on the inside.

Cool 1 minute, then remove with a spatula from cookie sheets to wire racks to cool completely. Makes 2 dozen.

Holiday Buffet Peppermint Dessert Squares

They'll rave about this one for a long time after the holidays are over. A truly divine dessert, deliciously rich and another no-bake wonder.

2 cups finely crushed chocolate wafer cookies

½ cup unsalted butter, melted and cooled, plus additional, melted, for brushing foil

3 tbsp. granulated sugar

1 cup coarsely chopped semisweet chocolate

⅔ cup heavy (whipping) cream

FILLING

1 cup confectioners' sugar, sifted

16 oz. cream cheese, room temperature

2 tsp. pure peppermint extract

1½ cups heavy (whipping) cream

¾ cup finely crushed peppermint candies, divided

BEV'S BITES

An 8 oz. package of chocolate wafer cookies will yield 2 cups.

Sometimes frozen items are difficult to cut. Let this pan of frozen delights sit at room temperature for 15 minutes, then cut with a knife repeatedly dipped in hot water (and carefully wiped between cuts) to make it a little easier to cut into squares.

Line a 13x9" baking pan with foil. Lightly brush bottom and sides of foil with melted butter.

In a medium bowl, combine the chocolate wafer cookie crumbs, butter, and sugar until blended. Press onto bottom of foil-lined pan. Set aside.

In a small saucepan, over low heat, combine the chocolate pieces and cream, stirring, until the chocolate is melted and the mixture is smooth. Pour over cookie crumb mixture. Set in freezer for 30 minutes.

For the Filling: Using an electric mixer, in a large bowl, combine the confectioners' sugar, cream cheese, and peppermint extract until smooth and fluffy. Scrape down sides and bottom of bowl.

In another bowl, whip heavy cream until firm peaks form. Gently fold cream and ½ cup of the crushed peppermint candies into the cream cheese mixture. Spread evenly over frozen layer and sprinkle with additional crushed candy. Cover lightly and freeze for at least 3 hours up to overnight.

Serve frozen or refrigerated; lifting the final product out in one piece with the aid of the foil, gently peel foil off bottom and cut into squares. Store any remaining squares in the freezer. Makes 2 dozen.

Cinnamon Macaroons

Ground cinnamon, the finest and freshest you can buy, will take these macaroons over the top.

2 large egg whites, room temperature
1/2 tsp. pure vanilla extract
2/3 cup granulated sugar
1 tsp. ground cinnamon
1 cup flaked sweetened coconut
1/2 cup finely chopped pecans, toasted
1 oz. bittersweet chocolate, finely grated

BEV'S BITES
These macaroons freeze beautifully for up to 2 months.

Heat oven to 325 degrees. Line cookie sheets with parchment paper.

Using an electric mixer, in a large bowl, combine the egg whites and vanilla. Beat mixture on high speed until soft peaks form.

In a small bowl, mix together the sugar and cinnamon.

With mixer on medium-high speed, add the sugar mixture to the egg white mixture, a tbsp. at a time, beating until stiff peaks form. Fold in coconut, pecans, and grated chocolate.

Drop by rounded teaspoonfuls, placing 2" apart on prepared cookie sheets. Bake about 20 to 22 minutes or until macaroons are set and dry. Cool 1 minute, then remove from cookie sheets to wire racks to cool completely. Makes about 1 1/2 dozen.

These Honey Gold Macaroons are simply elegant, but they'd taste just as delicious served on a paper plate.

Honey Gold Macaroons

Even the fussiest of macaroon eaters will love these honey golds loaded with two types of coconut. Just perfect with a cup of tea.

1 cup granulated sugar
3 tbsp. unbleached, all-purpose flour
1/4 tsp. salt
4 large egg whites, room temperature
1 tbsp. honey, clover, orange blossom, or your favorite local honey
1 tsp. pure vanilla extract
2 1/2 cups flaked sweetened coconut, "flaked" into separate pieces
2 cups unsweetened coconut, finely shredded or large flakes

BEV'S BITES

One of the best parts of this cookie (aside from the eating) is there are no worries about stiffly beaten egg whites and folding, folding, and more folding.

In a large bowl, stir together the sugar, flour, and salt. Add the egg whites, honey, and vanilla, whisking until smooth.

In another large bowl, stir together both types of coconut, mixing to blend.

Pour the egg white mixture over the coconut, stirring with a wooden spoon until evenly mixed. Cover and chill batter for 30 minutes.

Heat oven to 300 degrees. Line cookie sheets with parchment paper.

Drop batter by rounded tablespoonfuls on prepared cookie sheets, placing 2" apart. Bake for 15 to 19 minutes or until a light golden brown.

Cool 1 minute, then remove from cookie sheets to wire racks to cool completely. Makes 2 dozen.

Lacy Walnut Cookie Rolls

The baking and rolling of these take some getting used to even though the batter is very easy to make. Extra effort aside, these are very elegant cookies and are just right served with a scoop of sorbet for a perfect end to a perfect meal.

½ cup unsalted butter, room temperature
⅔ cup granulated sugar
½ cup light corn syrup
1 tbsp. pure vanilla extract
1 cup unbleached, all-purpose flour
¾ cup finely chopped walnuts, toasted

BEV'S BITES

After you make a few of these, you'll develop a rhythm and get the hang of rolling the cookies. You'll be an expert in no time at all!

Once you become an expert, you'll know it's best to work with only a few cookies at a time as they quickly become too crisp to roll. If you've become overly confident and the cookies do become too crisp to roll, return to oven for a few seconds to soften.

Heat oven to 350 degrees. Cut several pieces of foil into 6" squares and lightly grease. Line cookie sheets with 2 to 4 squares of foil per sheet.

In a small saucepan, melt the butter, sugar, corn syrup, and vanilla, stirring until butter melts and mixture is combined.

Remove from heat and mix in the flour and walnuts. Drop a slightly rounded teaspoonful of batter on the center of each square.

Bake for 7 to 9 minutes or until cookies are an even golden color. Remove from oven; let stand about 1 minute.

With a metal spatula, loosen edge of cookie from foil and peel off foil. *Quickly* roll each cookie around the handle of a wooden spoon to shape.

Working quickly, repeat with remaining cookies and regrease and reuse foil squares to bake remaining batter. Makes about 4 dozen.

You don't need to say much when you put a plateful of these Lacy Walnut Cookie Rolls on your table. Everyone will surely be impressed by your cookie talents.

Dainty Strips with Chocolate Chips

Crisp, delicate, and very different from traditional chocolate chip cookies, these strips of crunch and chocolate never made it very far after testing and photographing. Let the celebrating begin!

½ cup plus 6 tbsp. unsalted butter, room temperature
½ cup firmly packed light brown sugar
3 tbsp. firmly packed dark brown sugar
5 tbsp. granulated sugar
1½ tsp. pure vanilla extract
1 large egg
1½ cups unbleached, all-purpose flour
¼ tsp. baking powder
½ tsp. salt
6 oz. semisweet chocolate chips

BEV'S BITES

These cookies remind me of biscotti without the attitude!

Don't skimp on the quality of chocolate chips for this recipe. If you'd like a more intense chocolate flavor per bite, use bittersweet chocolate, chopped the size of chocolate chips.

A delicate, crisp version of everyone's favorite chocolate chip cookie, these Dainty Strips with Chocolate Chips help elevate that common cookie to a host's must-serve list.

Heat oven to 375 degrees. Line cookie sheets with parchment paper.

Using an electric mixer, in a large bowl, beat together the butter, brown sugars, and granulated sugar until light and fluffy. Scrape down sides and bottom of bowl.

Beat in the vanilla and egg until blended. Mix in the flour, baking powder, and salt, and then stir in the chocolate chips.

Form the dough into 4 equal strips, 8½" long. Place 2 strips of dough on each cookie sheet and flatten each to a width of 1½". Keep the strips of dough at least 4" apart as they spread during baking.

Bake for 15 to 18 minutes or just until the strips are a light golden color. Remove the baking sheets from the oven and immediately cut each strip on a diagonal into small strips, about 8 to 10 strips per side, cutting from the center of the strip up to the top, then down to the bottom. Cool completely on a wire rack. Makes about 2 dozen after you eat the ends.

Annette's Flowerpot Cookies

My friend and fellow baker, Annette Felton, is a preschool teacher.
Who better to create the perfect gift for any kid to give (or receive)?

BEV'S BITES ————————

Cookie sticks are similar to lollipop sticks, but they're thicker and therefore perfect for baking and holding a cookie in place. They're available at craft stores or bakery supply stores.

Edible gifts, such as this selection of Annette's Flowerpot Cookies, are perfect treats to make for Mother's Day or Grandparent's Day.

THE COOKIES

Roll out your favorite sugar cookie dough. Dough should be at least $1/4$" thick.

Cut using 4" cookie cutters to desired shapes.

On parchment-paper-lined cookie sheets, push a cookie stick 1" into the unbaked cutout cookie.

Bake according to recipe. Cool 1 minute, then remove from cookie sheets to wire racks to cool completely. Note that you want to use a spatula to remove the cookies from the cookie sheets—not by picking up the stick.

Frost and decorate as desired, making sure that the frosting and decorations are set before assembling the flowerpot.

THE FLOWERPOT

Fill a 6" clay flowerpot with pieces of Styrofoam cut to fit inside the pot.

Leave about 1" clearance at the top of the pot.

Using a glue gun, glue decorative ribbon around the rim and attach a bow at the front of the pot.

Gently push 5 to 7 cookies on a stick into the Styrofoam.

Use shredded green paper to cover up the Styrofoam (it should look like grass).

Give as a gift. Also makes a great centerpiece.

Spell a Name Sugar Cookies

Shape these sugar cookies into letters and numbers and names. Serve them at your next party. What fun to have your guests eat their words.

½ cup granulated sugar
½ cup unsalted butter, room temperature
3 oz. cream cheese, room temperature
1 tsp. pure vanilla extract
1⅔ cups unbleached, all-purpose flour
¼ tsp. salt
Granulated sugar for rolling

BEV'S BITES
If desired, decorate with colored sprinkles or sugars instead of the granulated sugar, or shape dough into pretzels.

Heat oven to 350 degrees.

Using an electric mixer, in a large bowl, beat together the sugar, butter, and cream cheese until well mixed. Scrape down sides and bottom of bowl.

Add vanilla; blend well.

Mix in the flour and salt. Scrape down sides and bottom of bowl.

Knead dough on a lightly floured surface just until smooth and no longer sticky.

Shape dough into ½" thick ropes and roll in granulated sugar. Form into letters, numbers, or other shapes as desired. Place shaped dough 2" apart on ungreased cookie sheets.

Bake for 8 to 12 minutes or just until edges are a light golden color. Cool 1 minute, then remove from cookie sheets to wire racks to cool completely. Makes about 2 dozen (obviously depending on the size of the letters and numbers).

FILLED COOKIES AND SCOOP AND DROP COOKIES

*These Dainty Chocolate Wafer Sandwiches are tiny, so
I believe that three counts as only one bite.*

Filled Cookies

With endless variations, filled cookies are like unexpected presents—wrapped around intrigue, layers of surprise, and (hopefully) the happiest of endings. (Pretty dramatic, huh?!)

The selections that fill this chapter will delight your taste buds and satisfy even the busiest of baker's needs to make something a little extra special.

A hint or two:

* Be sure fillings are set before moving cookies to prevent slippage and damage.

* Make cookies as uniform as possible, and the best way to do this is by using a cookie scoop for the batter.

Scoop and Drop Cookies

Mounds of soft dough scooped then dropped onto cookie sheets, these are some of the simplest cookies to make.

A hint or two:

* Once again, our cookie scoop comes to the rescue for uniformity in size and baking time.

* If dough is sticking to the scoop or spoon you're dropping it from, coat the scoop or spoon ever so lightly with oil for easier release.

Milk and Bittersweet Chocolate Sandwiches

A delightful chocolate cookie with a smear of chocolate in the center . . . bringing out the kid in all of us.

3 tbsp. unsalted butter, room temperature
½ cup granulated sugar
6 oz. coarsely chopped milk chocolate, melted and cooled
1 large egg
¾ tsp. pure vanilla extract
¾ cup unbleached, all-purpose flour
¾ tsp. baking powder
⅛ tsp. salt

CHOCOLATE SOUR CREAM FROSTING

3 oz. coarsely chopped bittersweet chocolate, melted and cooled
2 tbsp. unsalted butter, room temperature
¼ cup sour cream
1¼ cups confectioners' sugar, sifted

Using an electric mixer, in a large bowl, beat together the butter and sugar until well blended. Add the melted chocolate, egg, and vanilla, beating until combined. Scrape down sides and bottom of bowl.

Mix in the flour, baking powder, and salt. Divide dough in half and shape into 2 disks. Wrap in plastic wrap; flatten to ½". Chill dough for 1 hour.

Heat oven to 350 degrees.

Cut each disk in half and shape each piece of dough into a 9" log. Cut into ¼" thick slices, placing 1" apart on ungreased cookie sheets.

Bake for 8 to 10 minutes or just until edges of slices are set. Cool 1 minute, then remove from cookie sheets to wire racks to cool completely.

For the Frosting: Using an electric mixer, in a medium bowl, combine the melted chocolate, butter, and sour cream, beating just until combined. Scrape down sides and bottom of bowl.

Mix in the confectioners' sugar until Frosting reaches desired spreading consistency.

Spread a slight tsp. of filling carefully over the flat side of half of the cutouts. Top with remaining half of cutouts, flat side in. Gently press together and allow to set. Makes about 4 dozen.

Dainty Chocolate Wafer Sandwiches

These little babies are so flaky and delicate it seems as if you're not even eating them! They are perfect on a cookie tray.

½ cup unsalted butter, room temperature

2 tbsp. granulated sugar plus additional for dipping cutouts

4 tsp. half-and-half

1 oz. coarsely chopped unsweetened chocolate, melted and cooled

1 cup unbleached, all-purpose flour

FILLING

¾ cup confectioners' sugar, sifted

¼ cup unsalted butter, room temperature

1 tsp. strawberry jam, raspberry jam, or raspberry purée

BEV'S BITES

Oh, sure, you're not likely to have just a little half-and-half in your kitchen, but using milk just doesn't give you the richness these cookies deserve. Go ahead, splurge!

Using an electric mixer, in a large bowl, cream together the butter, sugar, and half-and-half until light and fluffy. Scrape down sides and bottom of bowl.

Add melted chocolate, blending until well mixed.

Mix in the flour until blended. Divide dough in half and shape into 2 disks. Wrap in plastic wrap; flatten to ½". Chill dough for 2 hours.

Heat oven to 400 degrees. Line cookie sheets with parchment paper.

Roll dough out on a lightly floured surface to ¼" thick, one disk at a time (keeping remaining dough refrigerated). Cut with small square scalloped-edge cookie cutters. Dip both sides of cutouts in additional sugar, placing 2" apart on prepared cookie sheets, pricking once or twice with a fork.

Bake for 6 to 7 minutes or just until cookies are set. Cool 1 minute, then remove from cookie sheets to wire racks to cool completely.

For the Filling: Using an electric mixer, in a medium bowl, combine the confectioners' sugar, butter, and jam or purée until light and fluffy. Scrape down sides and bottom of bowl.

Spread a slight teaspoon of Filling carefully over the flat side of half of the cutouts. Top with remaining half of cutouts, flat side in. Gently press together and allow to set. Makes about 4 dozen.

Peanut Butter Cocoa Delights

Filled with a peanut butter surprise, these cocoaliscious cookies will please anyone who loves a candy peanut butter cup.

½ cup unsalted butter, room temperature
½ cup granulated sugar
½ cup firmly packed light brown sugar
¼ cup creamy peanut butter
1 large egg
1 tbsp. milk, whole or 2 percent
1 tsp. pure vanilla extract
1½ cups unbleached, all-purpose flour
½ cup unsweetened cocoa powder, sifted
½ tsp. baking soda

FILLING

¾ cup confectioners' sugar, sifted
½ cup plus 2 tbsp. creamy peanut butter

½ cup granulated sugar

Heat oven to 350 degrees. Line cookie sheets with parchment paper.

Using an electric mixer, in a large bowl, beat together the butter, sugars, and peanut butter until light and fluffy. Scrape down sides and bottom of bowl.

Add egg, milk, and vanilla, beating until combined. Mix in the flour, cocoa powder, and baking soda. Scrape down sides and bottom of bowl.

Shape dough with cookie scoop into 32 balls, each about 1¼". Set aside on waxed-paper-lined tray.

For the Filling: Using an electric mixer, in a medium bowl, combine the confectioners' sugar and peanut butter, beating until smooth. Shape into 32 balls, each about ½" to ¾".

On lightly floured work surface, flatten a chocolate dough ball and top with peanut butter ball. Shape flattened dough over peanut butter ball, completely covering peanut butter ball and reshape into a ball. Repeat with remaining dough.

Place balls 2" apart on prepared cookie sheets and flatten with bottom of glass dipped in granulated sugar. Bake about 7 to 9 minutes or just until tops feel firm to the touch.

Cool 1 minute, then remove from cookie sheets to wire racks to cool completely. Makes about 2½ dozen.

*Even these Chocolate Filled-with-Peanut-Butter Wraparounds enjoy
seeing their own reflection . . . before being eaten!*

Chocolate Filled-with-Peanut-Butter Wraparounds

Not quite a peanut butter cup, not quite a cookie, and made extra rich with the addition of cream cheese—the best way to describe these cookies is "just plain good"!

½ cup firmly packed light brown sugar
¼ cup granulated sugar
½ cup unsalted butter, room temperature
6 oz. cream cheese, room temperature
1 tsp. pure vanilla extract
1 large egg
2 cups unbleached, all-purpose flour
¼ cup unsweetened cocoa powder, sifted
1 tsp. baking powder
½ cup creamy peanut butter
¼ cup confectioners' sugar, sifted

TOPPING

1 cup confectioners' sugar, sifted
1 tbsp. unsalted butter, room temperature
2 tbsp. unsweetened cocoa powder, sifted
2 tbsp. milk, whole or 2 percent
2 oz. cream cheese, room temperature

BEV'S BITES

Laugh if you must, but it's easiest to put the Topping on with clean hands—a little scoop and blob and a quick swirl—otherwise if you're not careful, the peanut butter filling will smear.

Heat oven to 350 degrees. Line cookie sheets with parchment paper.

Using an electric mixer, in a large bowl, cream the brown sugar and granulated sugar, butter, and cream cheese until light and fluffy. Scrape down sides and bottom of bowl.

Add in vanilla and egg. Mix in the flour, cocoa powder, and baking powder until blended. Scrape down sides and bottom of bowl.

In a small bowl, stir together the peanut butter and confectioners' sugar until smooth.

Shape dough into 1" balls, placing 2" apart on prepared cookie sheets. With your thumb, make an indentation in the center of each cookie, filling with ½ tsp. of the peanut butter mixture.

Bake for 9 to 11 minutes or just until cookie is firm to the touch.

Cool 1 minute, then remove from cookie sheets to wire racks to cool completely.

For the Topping: Using an electric mixer, in a small bowl, beat together the sugar, butter, cocoa powder, milk, and cream cheese until mixture is well blended and somewhere between a glaze and a frosting, not too thin yet not too thick.

Top cookies with Topping. Allow to set slightly. Makes about 4 dozen.

Chocolate-Filled Meringue Kisses

These didn't sit around long at our home . . . they were perfectly crispy with a wonderful chocolate center.

2 large egg whites, room temperature
$\frac{1}{2}$ tsp. pure vanilla extract
$\frac{1}{8}$ tsp. cream of tartar
$\frac{2}{3}$ cups granulated sugar
3 oz. coarsely chopped bittersweet chocolate

BEV'S BITES

Just to review, when whipping egg whites, soft peaks will have the tips curling; stiff peaks will stand straight.

A pastry bag and a large star tip will cost you almost nothing, and the final results will be well worth the minimal expense. You'll achieve professional-looking meringue kisses, and all your friends will surely have meringue envy.

If you must, an apricot fruit spread makes a nice alternative to the chocolate in the middle.

Heat oven to 300 degrees. Line cookie sheets with parchment paper.

Using an electric mixer, in a medium bowl, beat together the egg whites, vanilla, and cream of tartar until soft peaks form.

Beat in the sugar, a tbsp. at a time, until stiff peaks form.

Spoon whipped mixture into a pastry bag fitted with a large star tip. Pipe $1\frac{1}{2}$" diameter mounds about 2" apart onto prepared cookie sheets.

Bake for 15 to 20 minutes or until firm and bottoms are a very light golden brown. Do not underbake.

Cool 1 minute, then remove from cookie sheets to wire racks to cool completely.

In a double boiler, set over simmering (not boiling) water, melt the chocolate, stirring often, just until smooth. Remove top of double boiler and place on kitchen towel.

Spread a slight tsp. of melted chocolate carefully over the flat side of half of the meringues. Top with remaining half of meringues, flat side in. Gently press together and allow to set on waxed-paper-lined trays. Makes about $2\frac{1}{2}$ dozen.

*Strut your cookie-baking stuff with these
Chocolate-Filled Meringue Kisses.*

Little Almond Cookies Filled with White Chocolate

These are rich, with the subtle but sweet flavors of chocolate, both dark and white.

¾ cup unsalted butter, room temperature
½ cup confectioners' sugar, sifted
1 tsp. pure vanilla extract
1 large egg
1⅓ cups unbleached, all-purpose flour
¼ cup unsweetened cocoa powder, sifted
¼ tsp. salt
½ cup finely chopped almonds, toasted
Granulated sugar for rolling

FILLING

6 oz. coarsely chopped white chocolate
3 tbsp. heavy (whipping) cream
½ cup finely chopped almonds, toasted

Using an electric mixer, in a large bowl, beat together the butter and sugar until light and fluffy. Scrape down sides and bottom of bowl.

Add the vanilla and egg, beating to blend.

Mix in the flour, cocoa powder, and salt, and then stir in the almonds. Scrape down sides and bottom of bowl.

Cover and chill dough for 2 hours.

Heat oven to 350 degrees.

Shape dough into ¾" balls, rolling in granulated sugar to coat. Place on ungreased cookie sheets, and then press with the flat bottom of a glass to about 1" circles.

Bake for 6 to 8 minutes or just until tops are firm. Cool 1 minute, then remove from cookie sheets to wire racks to cool completely.

For the Filling: In a double boiler, set over simmering (not boiling) water, melt the white chocolate with the cream, stirring often, just until smooth. Remove top of double boiler and place on kitchen towel. Stir in the almonds.

Spread a slight tsp. of filling carefully over the flat side of half of the cookies. Top with remaining half of cookies, flat side in. Gently press together and allow to set. Makes about 2 dozen.

Coffee and Vanilla Sandwich Cookies

The perfect cookie for the coffee lover, crisp and flavorful.

½ cup granulated sugar
½ cup unsalted butter, room temperature
1 tbsp. milk, whole or 2 percent
1 tsp. pure vanilla extract
1 large egg
1¼ cups unbleached, all-purpose flour
1 tsp. cream of tartar
½ tsp. baking soda
¼ tsp. salt

FILLING

¼ cup instant espresso powder
4 tsp. hot water
2 tbsp. unsalted butter, room temperature
1⅓ cups confectioners' sugar, sifted
Just a drop of coffee extract, optional

Using an electric mixer, in a large bowl, beat together the sugar and butter until light and fluffy. Scrape down sides and bottom of bowl.

Add the milk, vanilla, and egg, blending until well combined.

Mix in the flour, cream of tartar, baking soda, and salt. Scrape down sides and bottom of bowl.

Divide dough in half and shape into 2 disks. Wrap in plastic wrap; flatten to ½". Chill dough for 2 hours up to overnight.

Heat oven to 400 degrees.

Roll dough out on a lightly floured surface to ⅛" thick, one disk at a time (keeping remaining dough refrigerated). Cut with a floured 1½" round cookie cutter, placing 1" apart on ungreased cookie sheets.

Bake for 4 to 5 minutes or just until edges are a light golden brown. Cool 1 minute, then remove from cookie sheets to wire racks to cool completely.

For the Filling: In a small bowl, combine the espresso powder with 4 tsp. hot water, whisking to blend.

Using an electric mixer, in a medium bowl, beat together the butter, confectioners' sugar, espresso powder mixture, and coffee extract just until desired spreading consistency is reached.

Spread a slight tsp. of Filling carefully over the flat side of half of the cutouts. Top with remaining half of cutouts, flat side in. Gently press together and allow to set. Makes about 4 dozen.

As if one type of ginger in a cookie wasn't good enough, here I've combined freshly grated ginger, ground ginger, and candied ginger for maximum effect. Bake these Three Ginger Cinnamon-Filled Sandwiches today.

Three Ginger Cinnamon-Filled Sandwiches

A soft ginger cookie with a cinnamon and pecan creamy, dreamy wonder of a middle. This cookie is bursting with flavor.

½ cup plus 5 tbsp. unsalted butter, room temperature
½ cup firmly packed light brown sugar
½ cup granulated sugar
¼ cup molasses
⅓ cup freshly grated ginger
1 large egg
1½ cups unbleached, all-purpose flour
1½ tsp. baking soda
½ tsp. salt
1¼ tsp. ground ginger
¼ tsp. ground cloves
1 tsp. ground cinnamon
1½ cups quick-cooking oats
⅓ cup minced candied ginger

FILLING

¾ cup unsalted butter, room temperature
¾ cup finely chopped pecans, toasted
1 tsp. ground cinnamon
2¼ cups confectioners' sugar, sifted

BEV'S BITES

My cookie tester's husband became creative and filled a few of these with ice cream, apparently creating a delicious alternate filling.

Using an electric mixer, in a large bowl, beat together the butter, sugars, molasses, fresh ginger, and egg until light and fluffy. Scrape down sides and bottom of bowl.

Mix in the flour, baking soda, salt, ground ginger, cloves, cinnamon, and oats, stirring to blend well. Stir in the candied ginger pieces.

Divide dough into 4 pieces. Shape each section of dough into a 9" log and roll on a long sheet of waxed paper or plastic wrap. Twist the ends to seal the cylinders of dough. Chill the dough for 4 hours up to overnight.

Heat oven to 350 degrees. Line cookie sheets with parchment paper.

Unwrap one log at a time and cut into ¼" thick slices, placing 1" apart on prepared cookie sheets. Bake for 6 to 7 minutes or just until they are golden in color. Cool 1 minute, then remove from cookie sheets to wire racks to cool completely.

Make the Filling: Using an electric mixer, in a large bowl, beat together the butter, pecans, cinnamon, and confectioners' sugar until smooth.

Spread a generous tsp. of Filling carefully over the flat side of half of the cookies. Top with remaining half of cookies, flat side in. Gently press together just enough to bring the filling to the edge of the cookie. Allow to set. Makes about 6 dozen.

Inside Out Banana Bread Sandwich Cookies

These are fun to make and fill the house with wonderful aromas while baking.

1 cup granulated sugar
1 cup unsalted butter, room temperature
1/2 cup 1/8" thick slices of ripe banana
2 1/3 cups unbleached, all-purpose flour
1/4 tsp. salt
1 tsp. pure vanilla extract
1/2 cup coarsely chopped pecans, toasted

FILLING

3 cups confectioners' sugar, sifted
1/3 cup unsalted butter, room temperature
1 tsp. pure vanilla extract
3 tbsp. milk, whole or 2 percent

BEV'S BITES

A number 60 cookie scoop with a 1 3/8" opening makes for uniformity and attractiveness in an otherwise great-looking cookie.

Heat oven to 350 degrees. Line cookie sheets with parchment paper.

Using an electric mixer, in a large bowl, beat together the sugar, butter, and banana until well mixed. Scrape down sides and bottom of bowl.

Mix in flour, salt, and vanilla until blended. Stir in pecans.

Shape dough into balls, placing 2" apart on prepared cookie sheets. Bake for 13 to 15 minutes or just until edges are a light golden brown. Cool 1 minute, then remove from cookie sheets to wire racks to cool completely.

For the Filling: Using an electric mixer, in a medium bowl, combine the confectioners' sugar, butter, vanilla, and milk until desired spreading consistency. Scrape down sides and bottom of bowl.

Spread a tablespoonful of Filling carefully over the flat side of half of the cookies. Top with remaining half of cookies, flat side in. Gently press together and allow to set. Makes about 1 1/2 dozen.

The way I see it you have two options: 1) Pull apart the Inside Out Banana Bread Sandwich Cookies and lick the middle first, or 2) Bite them for the full sandwich affect. (Hint: There is no correct answer.)

A decidedly crisp and delicate sandwich cookie bursting with the bright flavors of apricot filling. Apricot Jam Sandwiches anyone?

Apricot Jam Sandwiches

It's hard to describe how wonderful these melt-in-your-mouth filled cookies are—light as air and bursting with apricot sunshine. (Did I mention they're pretty, too?)

1 cup unsalted butter, somewhere
    between cold and room temperature
2 cups unbleached, all-purpose flour
$\frac{1}{3}$ cup heavy (whipping) cream
Granulated sugar for dredging

FILLING

$\frac{3}{4}$ cup apricot fruit spread
3 tbsp. unsalted butter, room temperature

BEV'S BITES —————————

One of my cookie testers said, "These cookies are delicious even before the apricot filling is added." You have to love a baker that sneaks a taste or two before the job is done.

Using an electric mixer, in a large bowl, combine the butter and flour and blend just until mixture resembles fine crumbs. Add the cream and blend until mixture forms a soft dough.

Divide dough in thirds and shape into 3 disks. Wrap in plastic wrap; flatten to $\frac{1}{2}$". Chill dough for 40 minutes to 1 hour.

Heat oven to 375 degrees.

Roll dough out on a lightly floured surface to $\frac{1}{8}$" thick, one disk at a time (keeping remaining dough refrigerated). Cut into $1\frac{1}{4}$" rounds.

In a shallow bowl, place a generous amount of granulated sugar and dredge each cutout on both sides before placing 1" apart on ungreased cookie sheets. Prick once or twice with a fork. Bake for 6 to 8 minutes or just until set (cookies will not brown). Cool 1 minute, then remove from cookie sheets to wire racks to cool completely.

For the Filling: In a small bowl, stir together the fruit spread and butter until mixture is well combined and spreadable.

Spread about $\frac{1}{2}$ tsp. of Filling carefully over the flat side of half of the cutouts. Top with remaining half of cutouts, flat side in. Gently press together and allow to set. Makes about 3 dozen.

Maple Cream Wafers

In this standout filled cookie, heavy cream makes these extra rich and pure maple extract and maple sugar bring the flavors of fall to your taste buds.

1 cup unsalted butter, room temperature
⅓ cup heavy (whipping) cream
½ tsp. pure maple extract
2 cups unbleached, all-purpose flour
4 tbsp. maple sugar

FILLING

¼ cup unsalted butter, room temperature
1 cup confectioners' sugar, sifted
1 tbsp. pure maple syrup
1 tsp. milk, whole or 2 percent

Using an electric mixer, in a large bowl, beat together the butter, cream, and maple extract until well blended.

Mix in flour until well combined. Scrape down sides and bottom of bowl. Divide dough in half and shape into 2 disks. Wrap in plastic wrap; flatten to ½". Chill dough for 2 hours.

Heat oven to 375 degrees.

Roll dough out on a lightly floured surface to ⅛" thick, one disk at a time (keeping remaining dough refrigerated). Cut with your favorite cookie cutters, placing 1" apart on ungreased cookie sheets pricking once or twice with a fork. Sprinkle with maple sugar.

Bake for 8 to 9 minutes or just until lightly puffed and golden around edges. Cool 1 minute, then remove from cookie sheets to wire racks to cool completely.

For the Filling: Using an electric mixer, in a medium bowl combine the butter, confectioners' sugar, maple syrup, and milk until light and fluffy. Scrape down sides and bottom of bowl.

Spread a slight tsp. of filling carefully over the flat side of half of the cutouts. Top with remaining half of cutouts, flat side in. Gently press together and allow to set. Makes about 2½ dozen.

Double Chocolate Walnut Delights

How do you make a chocolate chunk cookie even richer? Make the dough with the addition of cream cheese!

1 cup unsalted butter, room temperature
¾ cup firmly packed light brown sugar
½ cup granulated sugar
4 oz. cream cheese, room temperature
2 large eggs
2¼ cups unbleached, all-purpose flour
1 tsp. baking soda
1¾ cups coarsely chopped walnuts or
  pecans, toasted
2 oz. coarsely chopped white chocolate
7 oz. coarsely chopped bittersweet
  chocolate or milk chocolate

BEV'S BITES

Milk chocolate makes for a sweeter tasting cookie, so I personally prefer to use the bittersweet.

Heat oven to 350 degrees.

Using an electric mixer, in a large bowl, beat together the butter, sugars, and cream cheese until light and fluffy. Scrape down sides and bottom of bowl.

Add eggs, beating until combined. Mix in the flour and baking soda. Scrape down sides and bottom of bowl.

Stir in nuts and chocolate pieces. Drop dough by rounded tablespoonfuls, placing 2" apart on ungreased cookie sheets.

Bake for 8 to 11 minutes or just until edges are golden brown.

Cool 1 minute, then remove from cookie sheets to wire racks to cool completely. Makes 5 dozen.

Cocoa Walnut Brownie Cookies

If you underbake these cookies ever so slightly, they'll satisfy you with a crisp outside and a chewy inside.

½ cup unsalted butter, room temperature
½ cup firmly packed light brown sugar
½ cup granulated sugar
1 large egg
1 tsp. pure vanilla extract
1 cup unbleached, all-purpose flour
½ cup unsweetened cocoa powder, sifted
½ tsp. baking soda
¼ tsp. baking powder
¼ tsp. salt
¾ cup coarsely chopped walnuts, toasted

Heat oven to 350 degrees. Line cookie sheets with parchment paper.

Using an electric mixer, in a large bowl, beat the butter and sugars until light and fluffy. Scrape down sides and bottom of bowl.

Add the egg and vanilla, stirring until blended.

Mix in the flour, cocoa powder, baking soda, baking powder, and salt. Scrape down sides and bottom of bowl. Stir in the walnuts.

Drop by teaspoonfuls on prepared cookie sheets, placing 1½" apart. Bake for 10 minutes just until firm to the touch. Cool 1 minute, then remove from cookie sheets to wire racks to cool completely. Makes about 2½ dozen.

BEV'S BITES

These cocoa concoctions will puff up gently and settle down slightly when done. (Sounds like a few personalities I know.)

Chocolate Intensity

Lots of deep dark chocolate and not too much flour makes for an intensely flavored cookie. Its large size makes for a true chocolate lover's dream.

3 oz. coarsely chopped unsweetened chocolate
18 oz. coarsely chopped semisweet chocolate, divided
½ cup unsalted butter, room temperature
3 large eggs
1 cup plus 2 tbsp. granulated sugar
1 tbsp. pure vanilla extract
7 tbsp. unbleached, all-purpose flour
½ tsp. baking powder
¾ tsp. salt
1½ cups coarsely chopped walnuts, toasted
1½ cups coarsely chopped pecans, toasted

BEV'S BITES

Of course, you could make these a little smaller, but why bother? They'll be eaten just as fast!

Heat oven to 325 degrees.

In a double boiler, set over simmering (not boiling) water, melt the unsweetened chocolate, 9 oz. of the semisweet chocolate, and all of the butter, stirring often, just until smooth. Remove top of double boiler and place on kitchen towel.

Using an electric mixer, in a large bowl, beat the eggs with the sugar until pale yellow and creamy. Add the vanilla and chocolate mixture, beating until smooth. Scrape down sides and bottom of bowl.

Mix in the flour, baking powder, and salt just until combined. Do not overbeat. Stir in the remaining chocolate pieces, walnuts, and pecans.

Scoop out ⅓ cup measures of dough, placing them 3" apart on ungreased cookie sheets. Bake one cookie sheet at a time on middle rack in oven for 24 minutes or just until tops begin to crack. Do not overbake.

Cool completely on a wire rack. Makes about 1½ dozen.

Chunks of White Chocolate Cookies

Don't be fooled by what might be labeled as white chocolate without cocoa butter listed in the ingredients; you're simply eating sickeningly sweet confectioners' coating.

1 cup unsalted butter, room temperature
³/₄ cup granulated sugar
³/₄ cup firmly packed light brown sugar
3 large eggs
1 tsp. pure vanilla extract
2¹/₂ cups unbleached, all-purpose flour
1 tsp. baking powder
1 tsp. baking soda
¹/₂ tsp. salt
1 cup coarsely chopped almonds, toasted
¹/₂ cup coarsely chopped pecans, toasted
¹/₂ cup coarsely chopped walnuts, toasted
12 oz. coarsely chopped white chocolate

Heat oven to 350 degrees.

Using an electric mixer, in a large bowl, cream together the butter and sugars until light and fluffy. Scrape down sides and bottom of bowl.

Add eggs and vanilla, beating to combine. Mix in the flour, baking powder, baking soda, and salt. Scrape down sides and bottom of bowl.

Stir in the almonds, pecans, walnuts, and white chocolate pieces until mixed.

Drop dough by rounded tablespoonfuls, placing 2" apart on ungreased cookie sheets. Bake for 11 to 15 minutes or just until light golden brown.

Cool 1 minute, then remove from cookie sheets to wire racks to cool completely. Makes about 4 dozen.

Killer Chocolate Crackles

Most bakers have a favorite chocolate cookie that crackles on the top and is perfect with a tall cold one. This is mine. Got chocolate?

¼ cup unsalted butter
4 oz. coarsely chopped unsweetened chocolate
2 cups unbleached, all-purpose flour, divided
2 cups granulated sugar
4 large eggs
2 tsp. baking powder
½ tsp. salt
½ cup finely chopped pecans
Confectioners' sugar for rolling

In a small saucepan, melt the butter and chocolate over low heat, stirring, until melted and smooth. Set aside to cool.

Using an electric mixer, in a large bowl, combine the cooled chocolate mixture, 1 cup of the flour, sugar, eggs, baking powder, and salt. Beat until well combined. Scrape down sides and bottom of bowl.

Mix in remaining flour and pecans. Cover and chill dough for 2 hours up to overnight.

Heat oven to 300 degrees. Line cookie sheets with parchment paper.

Shape dough into 1" balls, roll in confectioners' sugar, and place 2" apart on prepared cookie sheets. Bake for 11 to 14 minutes or just until set.

Cool 1 minute, then remove from cookie sheets to wire racks to cool completely. Makes about 3½ dozen.

I love all-natural colors, and the chopped cranberries do a great job of staining and brightening the frosting in these Very Cran-Berry cookies.

Very Cran-Berry

A very pretty, soft cookie with the tart taste of cranberry will add a festive touch to any cookie tray or dessert plate.

½ cup granulated sugar
⅓ cup firmly packed light brown sugar
¼ cup unsalted butter, room temperature
2 cups unbleached, all-purpose flour
½ tsp. baking powder
½ tsp. baking soda
¼ tsp. salt
¼ cup fresh orange juice
1 large egg
½ tsp. pure vanilla extract
1 tbsp. fresh orange zest, finely grated
1½ cups finely chopped fresh or frozen cranberries, partially thawed
½ cup finely chopped, toasted walnuts, optional

FROSTING

2 cups confectioners' sugar, sifted
2 tbsp. finely chopped fresh or frozen cranberries, partially thawed
2 tbsp. fresh orange juice

Heat oven to 375 degrees. Line cookie sheets with parchment paper.

Using an electric mixer, in a large bowl, cream together the sugars and butter until light and fluffy. Scrape down sides and bottom of bowl.

Mix in flour, baking powder, baking soda, and salt. Beat in orange juice, egg, vanilla, and zest. Scrape down sides and bottom of bowl.

Stir in the cranberries and walnuts, if using. Drop dough by teaspoonfuls onto prepared cookie sheets, placing 1" apart.

Bake for 9 to 12 minutes or just until edges are a light golden brown. Cool 1 minute, then remove from cookie sheets to wire racks to cool completely.

For the Frosting: In a medium bowl, combine the confectioners' sugar, cranberries, and orange juice, stirring until mixture reaches desired spreading consistency. Using a small angled spatula, spread Frosting atop cookies. Allow to set. Makes about 4 dozen.

BEV'S BITES

Imagine how tasty and colorful these would be with pomegranate seeds substituted for the chopped cranberries.

Cranberry Shortbread Drops

These are melt-in-your-mouth good, and the texture is reminiscent of a shortbread cookie.

½ cup unsalted butter, room temperature
½ cup light olive oil
½ cup granulated sugar
½ cup confectioners' sugar, sifted
2 tsp. fresh orange zest, finely grated
1 tsp. pure vanilla extract
1 large egg
2 cups unbleached, all-purpose flour
½ tsp. baking soda
½ tsp. cream of tartar
¼ tsp. salt
½ cup fresh or frozen cranberries, chopped

Heat oven to 350 degrees.

Using an electric mixer, in a large bowl, beat together the butter, oil, and sugars until well blended. Scrape down sides and bottom of bowl.

Add zest, vanilla, and egg, beating well. Mix in flour, baking soda, cream of tartar, and salt until combined. Scrape down sides and bottom of bowl.

Stir in the cranberries. Drop dough by rounded teaspoonfuls, placing 2" apart on ungreased cookie sheets.

Bake for 12 to 15 minutes or just until bottom of cookies are a light golden brown. Cool 1 minute, then remove from cookie sheets to wire racks to cool completely. Makes about 2½ dozen.

Orange White Chocolate Cookies

Crisp yet chewy with hints of white chocolate and orange. A sophisticated yet simple cookie.

½ cup unsalted butter, room temperature
½ cup granulated sugar
¼ cup firmly packed light brown sugar
1 large egg
3 tbsp. orange juice concentrate, thawed
1⅔ cups unbleached, all-purpose flour
½ tsp. baking soda
½ tsp. cream of tartar
½ tsp. salt
6 oz. coarsely chopped white chocolate

CITRUS DRIZZLE

1¼ cups confectioners' sugar, sifted
2 tbsp. fresh orange zest, finely grated
4 to 5 tbsp. orange juice concentrate, thawed

Heat oven to 350 degrees. Line cookie sheets with parchment paper.

Using an electric mixer, in a large bowl, cream together the butter and sugars until mixture is light and fluffy. Scrape down sides and bottom of bowl.

Add the egg and orange juice concentrate, beating to combine. Mix in the flour, baking soda, cream of tartar, and salt. Scrape down sides and bottom of bowl.

Stir in the white chocolate. Drop dough by rounded teaspoonfuls, placing 2" apart on prepared cookie sheets. Bake for 8 to 12 minutes or just until a light golden color.

Cool 1 minute, then remove from cookie sheets to wire racks to cool completely.

For the Citrus Drizzle: In a small bowl, whisk together the confectioners' sugar and zest, then add the orange juice concentrate until desired consistency is reached. Glaze cookies. Allow to set. Makes about 2½ dozen.

Lightly Glazed Soft Lemon and Orange Cookies

I love soft, flavorful scoop and drop cookies, a simple treat that I can whip up in a hurry and will satisfy my craving for something special. These fit those exacting cookie criteria.

½ cup unsalted butter, room temperature
1 cup granulated sugar
1½ tbsp. fresh orange zest, finely grated
1 tbsp. fresh lemon zest, finely grated
1½ tsp. pure vanilla extract
1 large egg
½ cup plus 3 tbsp. sour cream
1½ cups plus 3 tbsp. unbleached, all-purpose flour
½ tsp. baking powder
½ tsp. baking soda
½ tsp. salt

GLAZE

1¼ cup confectioners' sugar, sifted
2 tbsp. unsalted butter, melted
1 tbsp. fresh orange juice
1 tbsp. fresh lemon juice

Heat oven to 375 degrees. Line cookie sheets with parchment paper.

Using an electric mixer, in a large bowl, beat together the butter and sugar until light and fluffy. Stir in the zests. Scrape down sides and bottom of bowl.

Add vanilla, egg, and sour cream, beating until well blended.

Mix in the flour, baking powder, baking soda, and salt. Scrape down sides and bottom of bowl.

Drop the batter by rounded tablespoonfuls, placing 2" apart on prepared cookie sheets.

Bake for 10 to 12 minutes or until the cookies are firm and just beginning to turn golden around the edges. Cool 1 minute, then remove from cookie sheets to wire racks to cool completely.

For the Glaze: In a medium bowl, whisk together the confectioners' sugar, butter, and juices until smooth.

Place the wire racks atop sheets of waxed paper and lightly glaze each cookie with a small angled spatula. Let stand until Glaze is set. Makes about 2 dozen.

Lemon Yogurt Drop Cookies

If you love a soft, tender, textured cookie this one is for you. You can add variety to the basic recipe by substituting a different flavored yogurt.

1 cup unsalted butter, room temperature
1½ cups granulated sugar
1 cup lemon yogurt, drained
1 tbsp. fresh lemon zest, finely grated
1 tsp. pure lemon extract
2 large eggs
3½ cups unbleached, all-purpose flour
2 tsp. baking powder
½ tsp. baking soda
½ tsp. salt
Granulated sugar for sprinkling

BEV'S BITES

I measure the yogurt in a dry 1 cup measure, not a liquid measure.

Heat oven to 350 degrees. Line cookie sheets with parchment paper.

Using an electric mixer, in a large bowl, combine the butter and sugar, beating until light and fluffy. Add the yogurt, zest, lemon extract, and eggs, blending well. Scrape down sides and bottom of bowl.

Mix in flour, baking powder, baking soda, and salt until well combined. Drop dough by rounded teaspoonfuls, placing 2" apart on prepared cookie sheets. Sprinkle with sugar.

Bake for 9 to 12 minutes or just until edges are a light golden brown. Cool 1 minute, then remove from cookie sheets to wire racks to cool completely. Makes about 4½ dozen.

Tropical Delight Cookies

A handful of paradise, these soft cookies are filled with pineapple, macadamia nuts, and coconut. Bring on the cool summer breezes and sounds of the ocean.

¾ cup granulated sugar
½ cup unsalted butter, room temperature
8 oz. can crushed pineapple packed in juice, well drained and patted dry
1 tsp. pure vanilla extract
1¾ cups unbleached, all-purpose flour
1 tsp. baking powder
⅔ cup coarsely chopped, roasted macadamia nuts
½ cup flaked sweetened coconut plus additional for sprinkling atop cookies

BEV'S BITES

Unsweetened coconut can be substituted for sweetened coconut to make a cookie just as satisfying and a little less sweet.

Heat oven to 350 degrees.

Using an electric mixer, in a large bowl, beat the sugar and butter until light and fluffy. Scrape down sides and bottom of bowl.

Add the pineapple and vanilla, beating until well mixed.

Mix in the flour and baking powder, and then add the nuts and coconut stirring to blend. Scrape down sides and bottom of bowl.

Drop dough by teaspoonfuls, placing 2" apart on ungreased cookie sheets. Sprinkle with additional coconut.

Bake for 12 to 14 minutes or until cookies are set. Cool 1 minute, then remove from cookie sheets to wire racks to cool completely. Makes 2½ dozen.

Chocolate Chip Coconut Meringues

Sometimes you're wondering what to do with those leftover egg whites. Now, at last the answer . . . when life gives you egg whites, make meringues!

1½ cups mini semisweet chocolate
    chips, divided
2 large egg whites, room temperature
Dash of salt
½ tsp. pure vanilla extract
½ cup granulated sugar
½ cup unsweetened coconut flakes

BEV'S BITES
Making these on a day that isn't so humid will help ensure a successful baking experience.

Heat oven to 350 degrees. Line cookie sheets with parchment paper.

In a double boiler, set over simmering (not boiling) water, melt 1 cup of the chocolate chips, stirring often, just until smooth. Remove top of double boiler and place on kitchen towel.

Using an electric mixer, in a medium bowl, beat the egg whites with the salt and vanilla until soft peaks form.

Gradually add the sugar a tbsp. at a time, beating continuously until stiff peaks form, being careful not to overbeat.

Gently fold in melted chocolate, remaining ½ cup chocolate chips, and coconut.

Drop dough by teaspoonfuls onto prepared cookie sheets. Bake for 9 to 13 minutes or until dry and set. Makes about 2 dozen.

Stuff 'Em Sour Cream Drops

I often stuff pitted dates with pecans and serve them with a cheese tray for dessert. I developed this cookie when I needed something to fill a sour-cream-based dough with . . . the stuffed dates have never been the same!

¼ cup unsalted butter, room temperature
¾ cup firmly packed light brown sugar
1 large egg
½ cup sour cream
1¼ cups unbleached, all-purpose flour
½ tsp. baking powder
½ tsp. baking soda
¼ tsp. salt
30 to 40 pecan quarters, toasted
1 lb. pitted dates

ICING

½ cup unsalted butter
2 cups confectioners' sugar, sifted
1 tsp. pure vanilla extract

Heat oven to 375 degrees.

Using an electric mixer, in a large bowl, beat together the butter and brown sugar until light and fluffy. Scrape down sides and bottom of bowl.

Add the egg and sour cream, mixing to blend.

Mix in the flour, baking powder, baking soda, and salt until combined. Scrape down sides and bottom of bowl. Stuff pecan pieces into dates, then stir in the stuffed dates.

Drop dough by rounded tablespoonfuls, placing 2" apart on prepared cookie sheets. Try to allow one date per cookie.

Bake for 10 to 12 minutes or until golden brown. Cool 5 minutes, then remove from cookie sheets to wire racks to cool completely.

For the Icing: In a medium saucepan, melt the butter over medium heat, stirring, until golden brown (being careful not to burn). Remove saucepan from heat and whisk in the confectioners' sugar and vanilla, adding water as needed to reach a thick, drizzle consistency.

Place wire racks atop waxed paper. Drizzle cookies with Icing and allow to set. Makes 4½ dozen.

Lightly browning the butter enhances the flavor of the icing that gets drizzled atop these Stuff 'Em Sour Cream Drops.

Since carrots are good for my eyesight, I can easily see that someone has taken a bite out of my Cream-Cheese-Frosted Carrot Cookie.

Cream-Cheese-Frosted Carrot Cake Cookies

If you love carrot cake, you'll love these cookies. As an added bonus, think of this: more frosting per bite!

¾ cup unsalted butter, room temperature
½ cup firmly packed light brown sugar
6 tbsp. granulated sugar
2 tsp. pure vanilla extract
2 large eggs
2 cups grated carrots, finely chopped
1 cup canned, crushed pineapple packed in juice, well drained and patted dry
2 cups unbleached, all-purpose flour
1 tsp. baking powder
¾ tsp. baking soda
½ tsp. salt
1½ tsp. ground cinnamon
½ tsp. ground allspice
½ tsp. freshly grated nutmeg
½ tsp. ground ginger

FROSTING

9 oz. cream cheese, room temperature
⅓ cup unsalted butter, room temperature
¾ cup confectioners' sugar, sifted
1 tsp. pure vanilla extract

Heat oven to 425 degrees. Line cookie sheets with parchment paper.

Using an electric mixer, in a large bowl, beat together the butter and sugars until light and fluffy. Scrape down sides and bottom of bowl.

Add the vanilla and eggs, stirring until blended. Add the carrots and pineapple, stirring until blended.

Mix in the flour, baking powder, baking soda, salt, cinnamon, allspice, nutmeg, and ginger until combined. Scrape down sides and bottom of bowl.

Drop by tablespoonfuls, placing 1½" apart on prepared cookie sheets. Bake for 11 to 13 minutes or just until set and lightly golden. Cool 5 minutes, then remove from cookie sheets to wire racks to cool completely.

For the Frosting: Using an electric mixer, in a large bowl, beat together the cream cheese, butter, confectioners' sugar, and vanilla until blended and smooth. Spread a generous amount of Frosting carefully over the top of each cookie. Makes about 3 dozen.

A Few More Grains Than Normal Cookies

If you're a multigrain person, or like to make your own breakfast cookies, these are for you. Studded with whole-wheat flour, wheat germ, and rolled oats, they make for a great alternative to an energy bar.

2/3 cup unsalted butter, room temperature
3/4 cup granulated sugar
1/2 cup firmly packed light brown sugar
1 large egg
1/3 cup canola or light olive oil
2 tbsp. honey, clover, orange blossom, or your favorite locally produced honey
1 tsp. pure vanilla extract
1/2 cup unbleached, all-purpose flour
3/4 cup whole-wheat pastry flour
1/2 cup toasted wheat germ
2 1/2 cups old-fashioned rolled oats (not quick cooking)
1/2 tsp. baking soda
1/2 tsp. ground cinnamon
2 cups finely chopped bittersweet or semisweet chocolate

Heat oven to 350 degrees.

Using an electric mixer, in a large bowl, beat together the butter and sugars until light and fluffy. Scrape down sides and bottom of bowl.

Add the egg, oil, honey, and vanilla, mixing until well blended. Mix in the flours, wheat germ, oats, baking soda, and cinnamon just until combined. Scrape down sides and bottom of bowl. Stir in the chocolate pieces.

Drop dough by generous tablespoonfuls, placing 2" apart on ungreased cookie sheets. With lightly floured hands, flatten dough slightly on sheets. Bake about 14 to 15 minutes or just until golden around edges. Cookies will still be slightly soft on top.

Cool 1 minute, then remove from cookie sheets to wire racks to cool completely. Makes about 1 1/2 dozen.

BEV'S BITES

If you'd like to make these larger, adjust your baking time for a little longer and adjust your expectations for the recipe's yield!

Flavors of Butterscotch Cookies

Another easy cookie with a moist, flavorful sour cream base and an irresistible butterscotch theme.

1½ cups firmly packed light brown sugar
½ cup unsalted butter, room temperature
2 large eggs
1 tsp. pure vanilla extract
8 oz. sour cream
2½ cups unbleached, all-purpose flour
1 tsp. baking soda
½ tsp. baking powder
½ tsp. salt
⅔ cup coarsely chopped walnuts, toasted

FROSTING

½ cup unsalted butter
3⅓ cups confectioners' sugar, sifted
1 tsp. pure vanilla extract
5 tsp. milk, whole or 2 percent

BEV'S BITES

Frosting or Icing? It's what you learned . . . they're basically the same sugary whipped concoction we all love.

Heat oven to 375 degrees. Line cookie sheets with parchment paper.

Using an electric mixer, in a large bowl, beat together the sugar and butter until light and fluffy. Scrape down sides and bottom of bowl.

Add the eggs, vanilla, and sour cream, stirring until well blended. Mix in the flour, baking soda, baking powder, and salt. Scrape down sides and bottom of bowl. Stir in the walnuts.

Drop dough by teaspoonfuls, placing 1½" apart on prepared cookie sheets. Bake for 9 to 12 minutes or just until edges are a light golden brown. Cool 1 minute, then remove from cookie sheets to wire racks to cool completely.

For the Frosting: In a medium saucepan, melt the butter over medium heat, stirring, until golden brown (being careful not to burn). Remove saucepan from heat. Whisk in the confectioners' sugar, vanilla, and milk.

Quickly frost cookies, adding a little more milk if frosting begins to stiffen. Allow cookies to set. Makes about 4½ dozen.

The Texture-of-Meringue Sugar Cookies

You'll love the bit of chewiness and meringuelike crispy texture in this easy to make sugar cookie.

½ cup unsalted butter, room temperature
½ cup shortening
2 cups granulated sugar
3 large egg yolks
½ tsp. pure vanilla extract
1 tsp. baking soda
1 tsp. cream of tartar
⅛ tsp. salt
1¾ cups unbleached, all-purpose flour

BEV'S BITES

These are so much fun . . . as you bite into one, you'll be asking yourself is it more like a meringue or a sugar cookie. Who cares? Just enjoy.

Heat oven to 300 degrees.

Using an electric mixer, in a large bowl, beat together the butter and shortening until combined. Stir in the sugar, beating until mixture is light and fluffy. Scrape down sides and bottom of bowl.

Add the egg yolks and vanilla, beating until combined. Mix in the baking soda, cream of tartar, salt, and flour. Scrape down sides and bottom of bowl.

Shape dough into 1" balls, placing 2" apart on ungreased cookie sheets. Bake for 12 to 14 minutes or just until edges are set. Do not overbake; do not let edges brown.

Cool 1 minute, then remove from cookie sheets to wire racks to cool completely. Makes about 3½ dozen.

BIBLIOGRAPHY

Corriher, Shirley O. *CookWise*. New York: William Morrow, 1997.

Herbst, Sharon T. *Food Lover's Companion*. 2d ed. Hauppauge, New York: Barron's Educational Series, 1995.

Shaffer, Bev. *Brownies to Die For!*. Gretna, Louisiana: Pelican Publishing Company, 2006.

Shaffer, Bev and John. *No Reservations Required*. Wooster, Ohio: The Wooster Book Company, 2003.

Riely, Elizabeth. *The Chef's Companion*. 2d ed. New York: John Wiley & Sons, Inc., 1999.

Which to taste first? Which to taste second?

The End.

INDEX